D1558430

The Civil War and Emancipation

Lucent Library of Black History

Other titles in this series:

The Civil War and Emancipation

Lucent Library of Black History

James A. Corrick

LUCENT BOOKS

A part of Gale, Cengage Learning

GALE
CENGAGE Learning

Detroit • New York • San Francisco • New Haven, Conn • Waterville, Maine • London

© 2008 Gale, a part of Cengage Learning

For more information, contact
Lucent Books
27500 Drake Rd.
Farmington Hills, MI 48331-3535
Or you can visit our Internet site at gale.cengage.com

LIBRARY OF CONGRESS CATALOGING-IN-PUBLICATION DATA

Corrick, James A.
  The Civil War and emancipation / by James Corrick.
    p. cm. — (Lucent library of Black history)
  Includes bibliographical references and index.
  ISBN-13: 978-1-4205-0008-0 (hardcover)
  1. Slaves—Emancipation—United States—Juvenile literature. 2. United States—History—Civil War, 1861–1865—Juvenile literature. 3. African Americans—History—To 1863—Juvenile literature. 4. African Americans—History—1863–1877—Juvenile literature.
  I. Title.
  E468.C785 2007
  973.7'415—dc22

2007023015

ISBN-10: 1-4205-0008-2

Printed in the United States of America
3 4 5 6 7 12 11 10 09 08

Contents

Foreword

It has been more than 500 years since Africans were first brought to the New World in shackles, and over 140 years since slavery was formally abolished in the United States. Over 50 years have passed since the fallacy of "separate but equal" was obliterated in the American courts, and some forty years since the watershed Civil Rights Act of 1965 guaranteed the rights and liberties of all Americans, especially those of color. Over time, these changes have become celebrated landmarks in American history. In the twenty-first century, African American men and women are politicians, judges, diplomats, professors, deans, doctors, artists, athletes, business owners, and home owners. For many, the scars of the past have melted away in the opportunities that have been found in contemporary society. Observers such as Peter N. Kirsanow, who sits on the U.S. Commission of Civil Rights, point to these accomplishments and conclude, "The growing black middle class may be viewed as proof that most of the civil rights battles have been won."

In spite of these legal victories, however, prejudice and inequality have persisted in American society. In 2003, African Americans comprised just 12 percent of the nation's population, yet accounted for 44 percent of its prison inmates and 24 percent of its poor. Racially motivated hate crimes continue to appear on the pages of major newspapers in many American cities. Furthermore, many African Americans still experience either overt or muted racism in their daily lives. A 1996 study undertaken by Professor Nancy Krieger of the Harvard School of Public Health, for example, found that 80 percent of the African American participants reported having experienced racial discrimination in one or more settings, including at work or school, applying for housing and medical care, from the police or in the courts, and on the street or in a public setting.

It is for these reasons that many believe the struggle for racial equality and justice is far from over. These episodes of discrimination threaten to shatter the illusion that America has completely overcome its racist past, causing many black Americans to become increasingly frustrated and confused. Scholar and writer Ellis Cose has described this splintered state in the following way: "I have done everything I was supposed to do. I have stayed out of trouble with the law, gone to the right schools, and worked myself nearly to death. What more do they want? Why in God's name won't they accept me as a full human being?" For Cose and others, the struggle for equality and justice has yet to be fully achieved.

In many subtle yet important ways the traumatic experiences of slavery and segregation continue to inform the way race is discussed and experienced in the twenty-first century. Indeed, it is possible that America will always grapple with the fallout from its distressing past. Ulric Haynes, dean of the Hofstra University School of Business has said, "Perhaps race will always matter, given the historical circumstances under which we came to this country." But studying this past and understanding how it contributes to present-day dialogues about race and history in America is a critical component of contemporary education. To this end, the Lucent Library of Black History offers a thorough look at the experiences that have shaped the black community and the American people as a whole. Annotated bibliographies provide readers with ideas for further research, while fully documented primary and secondary source quotations enhance the text. Each book in the series explores a different episode of black history; together they provide students with a wealth of information as well as launching points for further study and discussion.

Battling for Emancipation

In 1860 some 4 million African Americans labored as slaves in the United States. Within six years all of these millions had been emancipated, that is, freed, and slavery was forever ended in the nation. This emancipation was a direct result of the Civil War (1861–1865), the four-year struggle between the slave-free North and the slaveholding South. During the latter years of the war, emancipation became both a Northern tool to achieve victory and a desired outcome of the war. Many in the North, from President Abraham Lincoln to the soldier in the field, came to believe that only by eliminating slavery would the nation once more be united. As the historian Ira Berlin and his colleagues write, "The beginning of the Civil War was the beginning of the end of slavery in the American South."[1]

To Abolish Slavery

The desire to end slavery predated the United States. Thomas Jefferson, himself a slaveholder, tried unsuccessfully to place a section in the Declaration of Independence condemning slavery and the international slave trade. Other slaveholders, such as

Jefferson's fellow Virginian George Washington and the first chief justice of the Supreme Court, John Jay of New York (where slavery was legal until 1827), called for an end to slavery. These critics felt that slavery not only demeaned the slave but also corrupted the owners, who treated other human beings as property. They also believed that slavery was at odds with the U.S. concept of individual liberty.

Although Jefferson would be unable to bring himself to free his slaves, both Washington, on his death, and Jay, during his lifetime, freed theirs. Although others followed Washington and Jay, particularly in the North, no widespread emancipation followed. Indeed, most Southern slaveholders not only retained their slaves but whenever possible increased the number of African Americans they owned. Emancipation did come to the North, where slavery had never been very popular. Still, most Northerners had little interest in ending Southern slavery, even though many of them disliked the institution.

Thomas Jefferson writes the Declaration of Independence. Jefferson wanted to add a condemnation of slavery to the document, but it was never approved.

Therefore, prior to the Civil War, Southern practice and Northern attitudes made emancipation seem like a distant prospect even to the most fervent of antislavery activists, or abolitionists. These activists were often tireless in their efforts to end slavery, illustrating through their writing and speeches the grim reality of slave life and ceaselessly calling for emancipation. Their efforts more often met with ridicule and hostility, both in the North and in the South. So despite their efforts, the abolitionists of prewar America were unable to bring an end to slavery.

Slavery and the Constitution

In addition to apathy and hostility, a major stumbling block to emancipation was the U.S. Constitution, which legally recognized slavery and protected the interests of slave owners, even calling for the return of fugitive slaves to their masters. Despite never using the words *slave* or *slavery*, the Constitution makes many references to both. As Michael Vorenberg notes:

> The word "slavery" did not appear in the Constitution of 1787—the framers opted for the less offensive expression "person held to service of labor"—but the institution nonetheless permeated the document. In five places slavery was directly indicated, and in as many as ten others it was implied. . . . Of the implicit concessions to slavery, the most important was the absence of any mention of congressional authority over slavery in the enumeration of congressional powers.[2]

Congress, being restricted to those powers actually listed in the Constitution, thus could not abolish slavery, even had it been able to do so in the face of resistance by representatives of the slave states in the House and Senate. In truth, because slavery was recognized and accepted by the Constitution, most Americans thought that none of the branches of the federal government—legislative, executive, or judicial—could decree emancipation.

Calls for Emancipation

Such an obstacle, however, did not keep the abolitionists from seeking emancipation. Some slavery opponents believed that the

Constitution should be scrapped in favor of a new charter that prohibited slavery. The abolitionist William Lloyd Garrison called the Constitution "a covenant with death and an agreement with Hell" before burning a copy and adding, "so perish all compromises with tyranny."[3]

Others called for the president or Congress to abolish African American servitude, despite the dubious constitutionality of such action. Still others felt that slaveholders should be encouraged to free their slaves by paying owners for their slaves. A few, such as John Brown, favored helping slaves to revolt and take their freedom by force. Almost none voiced the idea of amending the Constitution to achieve emancipation. Such an amendment would require the approval of three-fourths of the states in a country where half the states had slavery.

None of these proposals proved practical. None had even the support of the majority of Northerners, let alone Southerners. In time, some abolitionists, in despair of ever being able to promote emancipation, believed that the northern states should secede, and these states at least could then form a country free of slavery.

War and Slavery

Thus matters stood on the eve of the Civil War. However, although abolitionist efforts had not resulted in any real progress toward emancipation, they did convince eleven southern states—Virginia, North Carolina, South Carolina, Georgia, Florida, Alabama, Mississippi, Tennessee, Louisiana, Arkansas, and Texas —that slavery would eventually be abolished in the United States. These states consequently seceded and joined together to form the Confederate States of America.

The war that ensued did not start for the North as a crusade to end slavery. Abraham Lincoln was interested first and foremost in returning the Southern breakaway states to the Union. He was even willing to tolerate slavery in a restored United States, even though he personally despised the institution. Berlin and his colleagues observe that

> with President Abraham Lincoln in the fore, federal authorities insisted that the nascent [newly born] conflict must be a war to restore the national union, and nothing

CHARLESTON

MERCURY

EXTRA:

Passed unanimously at 1.15 o'clock, P. M. December 20th, 1860.

AN ORDINANCE

To dissolve the Union between the State of South Carolina and other States united with her under the compact entitled "The Constitution of the United States of America."

We, the People of the State of South Carolina, in Convention assembled, do declare and ordain, and it is hereby declared and ordained,

That the Ordinance adopted by us in Convention, on the twenty-third day of May, in the year of our Lord one thousand seven hundred and eighty-eight, whereby the Constitution of the United States of America was ratified, and also, all Acts and parts of Acts of the General Assembly of this State, ratifying amendments of the said Constitution, are hereby repealed; and that the union now subsisting between South Carolina and other States, under the name of "The United States of America," is hereby dissolved.

THE

UNION

IS

DISSOLVED!

An 1860 poster proclaims that the Union is dissolved. During the Civil War, the abolition of slavery became a goal for the North.

more. Confederate leaders displayed a fuller comprehension of the significance of slavery, which [Confederate] Vice-President Alexander Stephens called the cornerstone of the Southern nation.[4]

By the second year of the war, however, for political and military reasons, emancipation became a major goal for the North, even in the face of opposition from the slaveholding states of Missouri, Kentucky, Maryland, and Delaware that had stayed in the Union and from many non-slaveholding Northerners. By seeking emancipation, the North provided a strong moral foundation for its efforts to defeat the South as well as undermine the South's main source of labor. In the end, Union battlefield successes paved the way for the final emancipation of all African Americans.

Still, this recognition of the need for emancipation was not easy or quick in coming. To the antislavery activists, emancipation often seemed as distant as it had through the decades preceding the North-South conflict.

Chapter One

Abolitionists, Slaveholders, and Emancipation

In the first half of the nineteenth century, slavery grew rapidly in the South, where it became an integral part of the economy and the society. Opposing slavery, mostly in the North, was an active abolitionist movement. The issue of slavery proved increasingly divisive in the decades before the Civil War, with the most passionate abolitionists seeking an immediate end to slavery, while others sought merely to restrict its spread into the West. At the same time, proslavery factions sought with equal vigor to preserve and extend the slaveholding region of the nation.

Slavery's Long History

By the beginning of the Civil War, African American slavery extended back almost 250 years, predating the formation of the United States by a century and a half. In 1619 the first black slaves had arrived at the British colony of Jamestown in Virginia, and by the 1680s slaves were providing much of the labor on most large Virginian farms, or plantations. Other Southern colonies also came to depend heavily upon slave labor. Some of these enslaved people acted as house servants, but the majority worked the fields, clearing, plowing, planting, and harvesting.

African Americans also toiled in slavery in many of the Northern colonies. Nevertheless, the large agricultural estates of the South were rare in the North, where most farms were small and family owned and run. Thus Northern slavery was never very great or widespread, with most labor being done by paid workers. Consequently, by 1830 slavery had died out in the North, with most Northern states having passed laws abolishing it.

Slavery in the South

Slave numbers in the Southern states, however, continued to grow, and the institution, which came to be known by Southerners as "our peculiar institution," became increasingly important to

Slaves began arriving in Virginia in 1619.

the Southern economy. By 1860 enslaved African Americans made up over a third of the Southern population of 9 million, slave numbers having more than tripled since 1800. By contrast, the North's free black population was a half million in a total population of 23 million (there were also some half million free African Americans in the Southern states).

The growth of Southern slavery was fueled in large part by a need for a substantial workforce to raise cotton, which had become the dominant Southern crop in the early nineteenth century. Slaves were also used to raise other crops, for instance tobacco and rice, and although these other crops could be lucrative, it was cotton that was king in Southern agriculture. By mid-century, cotton made up almost 60 percent of all U.S. exports and accounted for 80 percent of all the cotton grown in the world. It went to factories in Great Britain, France, and other European countries, as well as to those in New England, where it was made into cloth and clothing. The crop was so profitable that, when in 1857 the rest of the United States reeled under an economic depression, the South remained economically untouched and prosperous.

Southern Attitudes Toward Slavery

Most of the Southern wealth was in the hands of a few plantation owners, those who could afford large numbers of slaves. Slaves were expensive, and not many whites in the South could afford them. Indeed, most of the estimated 350,000 slave owners had fewer than five slaves. Only 1,800 of them, all plantation holders, owned more than one hundred slaves.

Still, most whites in the South favored slavery. Small farmers, as author Steven E. Woodworth observes,

> considered [slavery] a beneficial and indispensable feature of the great order of the universe. They fully approved of the South's "peculiar institution" and hoped to make it into the ranks of the slaveholders themselves someday. They might well have relatives who were slaveholders and felt themselves connected to the slaveholding strata [class] of society by many ties, not the least of which was simply their common whiteness.[5]

16

Frederick Douglass

■

Born into slavery in Maryland, Frederick Douglass (1817–1895) was taught to read in defiance of state law by his owner's wife. He gained further education by talking with local white schoolboys. Beginning at age sixteen, he worked first as a field hand and then as a shipyard laborer. In 1838 he managed to escape, settling in New Bedford, Massachusetts.

His role as an active abolitionist began in 1841 when he was asked to speak at an antislavery convention. His eloquent and forceful speech immediately brought him further speaking engagements. He also began writing for abolitionist publications such as William Lloyd Garrison's the *Liberator*. In 1845 he published his autobiography, later revised in 1882 as *The Life and Times of Frederick Douglass*. From 1847 to 1860 he published the antislavery *North Star*, in which he campaigned for emancipation and African American civil rights.

During the Civil War, he met with Lincoln and urged immediate freeing of all slaves, the enlistment of blacks in the military, and the guarantee of full citizenship rights to former slaves. After the war he continued the fight for civil rights. During this postwar period, he held a number of government posts, the last being ambassador to Haiti (1889–1891).

Former slave Frederick Douglass's speeches and autobiography rallied people against slavery.

Those who did not own slaves dreamed of making enough money to buy a slave to help them raise more cash crops, which could provide enough income to allow the purchase of more land and more slaves. Such an expansion could eventually lead to entry into the ranks of the plantation-owning elite.

Even many of those who never expected to own a slave favored the institution because it made them part of the dominant class. No matter how poor a Southern white was, he or she still had more social standing than the millions of African American slaves.

Southern Justification of Slavery

The wealth of the plantation owners made them the dominant political force in the South, and they used their clout to stifle any attempt to abolish slavery. Emancipation would leave slaveholders without a workforce with which to bring in their crops. It would lead, they feared, to their impoverishment and indeed to that of the entire South. Slavery in their view was thus crucial to the Southern economy.

Additionally, they and many non-slaveholding whites offered a number of other justifications for slavery. They pointed out that slavery was found in the Bible, and thus they reasoned that it

A Roman lady is attended by her slaves. Southerners justified owning slaves by arguing that many ancient cultures also participated in the practice.

must be ordained by God. They also argued that many other cultures throughout history had slaves, among them the ancient Greeks and Romans. Further, the slavery advocates went on, the North filled its factories with wage slaves, who Southerners claimed were more poorly treated and worked in worse conditions than their African American slaves.

Southerners also defended slavery by asserting that it had rescued blacks from savage Africa, giving them security and exposing them to Christianity. In a like vein, Southern whites alleged that blacks were too childlike and unintelligent to lead lives without the supervision offered by slavery and their white masters. Many slave owners further claimed that African American slaves recognized the supposed benefits of slavery and were happy with their lot and did not wish to be free.

The Abolitionists

In the North many white Northerners held opinions about African Americans that were similar to those found in the South. Many white Northerners were either indifferent to slavery or openly hostile toward the idea of emancipation. Among the latter, small-town merchants saw free blacks as business rivals, while laborers and small farmers viewed them as competitors for jobs and farmland, respectively.

Still, there was a vocal minority of whites in the North who opposed slavery, most notably in the New England states and in particular Massachusetts. And as slavery grew in the South, so did opposition to it in the North. By the 1830s these Northern slavery opponents were organizing abolitionist societies to seek an end to the institution. These societies turned out newspaper articles, pamphlets, and books and sponsored conferences and public talks. All of these efforts were designed to publicize the plight of slaves in the hope that such depictions would lead to a groundswell of outrage that would eventually culminate in universal emancipation.

The South did have its own homegrown abolitionists, but they were unable to organize in the face of the political power of the slave-owning elite and the general acceptance of slavery by most Southerners. In fact, many Southern states such as South Carolina passed laws forbidding discussions either in print or in person of abolitionism and emancipation. Many Southern abolitionists were thus silenced, while others, after receiving death threats, fled north.

Demanding Immediate Emancipation

One of the most influential Northern abolitionists was William Lloyd Garrison of Massachusetts. In 1831 he founded the *Liberator*, an abolitionist newspaper that he would publish for decades and in which he would crusade for total emancipation. Two years later he helped establish the American Antislavery Society.

Garrison was famous among abolitionists and infamous among slavery advocates for the harshness and unrelenting nature of his criticism. He attacked slavery, slaveholders, and anyone whom he thought either actively or passively supported slaveholding—indeed anyone who did not seek an immediate end to slavery. As he wrote, "if those who deserve the lash feel it and wince at it, I shall be assured that I am striking the right persons in the right place."[6]

Garrison's purpose was to persuade others that slavery was a sin against the enslaved and that it corrupted the enslaver. Thus the only proper course of action was to end slavery immediately.

Other abolitionists such as Wendell Phillips joined Garrison in demanding an immediate end to slavery. Phillips was one of the most outspoken champions not only of emancipation but also of granting freed African Americans citizenship and full civil rights. His position was popular with many abolitionists.

Not all abolitionists favored Phillips's civil rights agenda. Nor did all seek immediate emancipation. Another early abolitionist, Theodore Weld, for instance, preferred a gradual ending of slavery through legislative action, particularly in the South. Garrison and Phillips had nothing but contempt for this approach, which they believed would never lead to emancipation but only to the continuation of slavery. They also disliked the gradualists' proposal of paying slave owners to free their slaves. To Garrison and Phillips, such payment was nothing more than a reward for owning slaves.

African Americans and Abolition

Many Northern African Americans were also active in the abolitionist movement. Both those born free and those escaped from slavery urgently wanted to see their fellow African Americans re-

I Will Be Heard

■

The abolitionist William Lloyd Garrison believed slavery should be abolished, going so far as to call the Constitution "a covenant with death and an agreement with Hell."

Among the most influential and determined abolitionists was William Lloyd Garrison, who in the January 1, 1831, issue of his antislavery newspaper the *Liberator* stated that he did not intend to muffle either his ideas or his language. Garrison wrote:

I am aware that many object to the severity of my language; but is there not cause for severity? I *will be* as harsh as truth, and as uncompromising as justice. On this subject [slavery], I do not wish to think, or speak, or write, with moderation. No! no! Tell a man whose house is on fire to give a moderate alarm; tell him to moderately rescue his wife from the hands of the ravisher; tell the mother to gradually extricate her babe from the fire into which it has fallen; but urge me not to use moderation in a cause like the present. I am in earnest—I will not equivocate—I will not excuse—I will not retreat a single inch—AND I WILL BE HEARD.

Quoted in William E. Cain, ed., *William Lloyd Garrison and the Fight Against Slavery: Selections from the* Liberator. New York: St Martin's, 1995, pp. 71–72.

leased from bondage. Therefore, they supported abolitionist efforts with money and volunteerism—the majority of the subscribers to Garrison's *Liberator* were black. Additionally, Northern African Americans held their own meetings, such as the National Negro Convention held in Philadelphia in 1830, and created their own organizations, like the American Society of Free Persons, also founded in 1830.

In the three decades preceding the Civil War, a number of prominent black abolitionists would emerge, such as William Wells Brown, Sojourner Truth, and Harriet Tubman. One of the earliest African American abolitionists was David Walker, a free black from North Carolina who migrated to Boston, where in September 1829 he published the *Appeal*. Walker's writing was avidly read by African Americans, particularly those enslaved in the South. The latter were provided with copies smuggled into almost every Southern state by sailors and other travelers to the South. The demand for the publication was so great that Walker put out a second and a third edition over the next nine months.

In the *Appeal* Walker sought to instill pride in his black readers and called on them to resist slavery, even if it meant killing those who oppressed them:

> They [slave owners] want us for their slaves, and think nothing of murdering us in order to subject us to that wretched condition—therefore, if there is an *attempt* made by us, kill or be killed. Now, I ask you, had you not rather

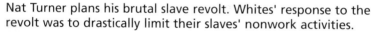

Nat Turner plans his brutal slave revolt. Whites' response to the revolt was to drastically limit their slaves' nonwork activities.

be killed than to be a slave to a tyrant, who takes the life of your mother, wife, and dear little children? Look upon your mother, wife, and children, and answer God Almighty; and believe this, that it is no more harm for you to kill a man, who is trying to kill you, than it is for you to take a drink of water when thirsty; in fact, the man who will stand still and let another murder him, is worse than an infidel, and, if he has common sense, ought not to be pitied.[7]

Nat Turner's Rebellion

William Lloyd Garrison found much to praise in the *Appeal*, but he could not accept its call for violence and open rebellion. As was true of many abolitionists, he was a pacifist, and he greeted the idea of slave insurrections with horror.

Garrison was not the only one horrified by the idea of slave revolts: Southern whites feared such rebellions, no matter how often they might claim that African Americans were happy in slavery. There had been insurrection plots in the past, and in 1831 the Virginia slave Nat Turner led a small band in revolt, killing over fifty whites before he was captured and executed. Southerners blamed the *Appeal* and other abolitionist writings for sparking the insurrection.

Southern response to the Turner revolt was to limit slave non-work activity as much as possible. Many Southern states passed laws forbidding slaves from learning to read and write, thus reducing the ability of slaves to read smuggled abolitionist literature and to communicate with each other over distances. Southern free blacks also suffered, their ability to travel or to assemble in large groups being severely restricted.

Aiding the Fugitive

David Walker died mysteriously the year before Nat Turner's rebellion. Some claimed that he had been poisoned by enraged Southerners, others that he had perished from tuberculosis as had his daughter.

Whatever the truth behind Walker's death, other African Americans were ready to step forward and work for emancipation. Although seldom going as far as Walker in encouraging the killing of slaveholders, many took more direct action than their white counterparts, hiding, feeding, and clothing escaped slaves whenever possible. They also helped organize the Underground Railroad that helped fugitive slaves leave the South for the North or for Canada. Harriet Tubman became famous for helping hundreds pass along the Underground Railroad to freedom.

A number of white abolitionists also helped fugitive slaves. In particular, many of the stations on the Underground Railroad were farms owned by whites, many by Quakers.

Abolitionist Writings

Of all the African American abolitionists, the most famous was Frederick Douglass, a largely self-taught fugitive slave until he was able to earn enough money to buy his freedom. Asked to describe his experiences as a slave at an abolitionist convention in 1841, he discovered a knack for public speaking. He also proved to be an effective writer, and his autobiography *Life and Times of Frederick Douglass* was one of the major antislavery tracts of prewar America.

The *Life and Times* joined the equally popular *American Slavery as It Is* by Theodore Weld. This 1839 best seller—it sold over one hundred thousand copies in its first year—detailed the horrors of slave life, with most of the book being taken from articles in Southern newspapers.

The impact of Douglass's and Weld's books paled in comparison to that of Harriet Beecher Stowe's *Uncle Tom's Cabin*, which was published in 1852. Stowe's book sold three hundred thousand copies in its first year and became an international bestseller. In this novel Stowe has her slave hero, Uncle Tom, suffer cruelly at the hands of his owner, Simon Legree. Although often criticized even at the time as sentimental and preachy, *Uncle Tom's Cabin* stirred many Northern readers and gained many recruits to the abolitionist movement.

Southern reaction to Stowe's novel was no less marked, although extremely hostile to this attack on their peculiar institution. As the scholar James M. McPherson writes, "The vehemence of southern denunciations of Mrs. Stowe's 'falsehoods' and 'distortion' was perhaps the best gauge of how close they hit home."[8] So great was the anger in the South that people went to prison for possessing a copy: Thus Marylander Samuel Green was sentenced to ten years for reading the novel.

An illustration from *Uncle Tom's Cabin* depicts Tom's sale at a slave market. The book won many converts to the antislavery cause.

Impact of the Abolitionists

Despite the popularity of books such as *Uncle Tom's Cabin*, the abolitionists made no real progress toward abolishing slavery in the United States during the decades leading up to the Civil War. Vocal though they were, they were a minority whom many Northerners disliked for their radical social ideas and for the fierceness of their condemnation of slavery and slave owners. They were despised almost as much in the North as in the South. Mobs of angry Northern workers, fearing that their jobs would be threatened by cheap black labor, sometimes broke up abolitionist meetings, occasionally beating participants badly.

Still, abolitionist publications and speeches kept chipping away at slavery, and if nothing else, they kept the issue of black bondage in the public eye. By doing so, they were seen in the South as a constant threat to slavery. Southerners reacted by defending slavery in print and speech. They also took political action.

In addition to state and local suppression of abolitionist doctrines and writings, Southerners depended upon their congressional representatives in the House and Senate to ensure that no federal legislation passed that interfered with slavery.

Compromising with Slavery

On one issue, abolitionists and Northern non-abolitionists generally agreed: keeping slavery from spreading west of the Mississippi River. The non-abolitionists who insisted that slavery be confined to the already-settled Southern states were known as Free-Soilers from the short-lived Free-Soil Party (1848–1854). Free-Soilers believed that the West should be developed by free labor rather than slave labor. They did not want to compete with

This map shows the divisions established by the Missouri Compromise of 1820.

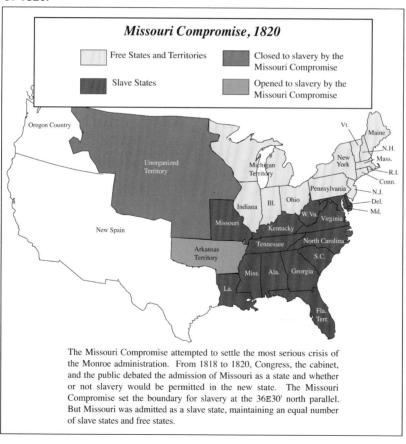

Missouri Compromise, 1820

Free States and Territories

Slave States

Closed to slavery by the Missouri Compromise

Opened to slavery by the Missouri Compromise

The Missouri Compromise attempted to settle the most serious crisis of the Monroe administration. From 1818 to 1820, Congress, the cabinet, and the public debated the admission of Missouri as a state and whether or not slavery would be permitted in the new state. The Missouri Compromise set the boundary for slavery at the 36E30' north parallel. But Missouri was admitted as a slave state, maintaining an equal number of slave states and free states.

slaves—or for that matter free blacks—for work, nor with slave-holders for land in the western territories.

Southerners were equally determined to see slavery in the West. Many Southerners feared that if slavery were banned from this region and portions of it entered as non-slaveholding, or free, states, the slave states would soon be outnumbered and lose political power. Indeed, if enough free states entered the Union, they might be able to declare slavery at an end in the United States by overriding, through sheer numbers, Southern representatives and senators.

Yet neither pro- nor antislavery factions were able to dictate policy in the West. Rather a series of congressional acts, beginning with the 1820 Missouri Compromise, tried to balance the interests of both sides. The Missouri Compromise allowed for the admission of slaveholding Missouri, which was part of the western territory bought from France in the 1803 Louisiana Purchase and which was settled mostly by Southerners. To maintain the free/slave balance, antislavery Maine was also admitted. Additionally, the Compromise split the remaining territory into slave and free, the dividing line running west from Missouri's southern border. North of that line, with the exception of Missouri, was free, while south of the line was slave.

The Compromise of 1850

In 1848 the U.S.-Mexican War added new western land to the country. The slave/free balance was maintained by having Texas (slave) and California (free) admitted. But instead of extending the old boundary line westward, Congress decided in the Compromise of 1850 to allow the territorial legislatures of the remainder of the land acquired from Mexico to vote on whether to be slave or free. Known as the New Mexico Territory, this land would later form the states of Arizona and New Mexico.

The Compromise of 1850 also strengthened a 1793 Fugitive Slave Act that allowed owners to retrieve runaway slaves from Northern states. The new version of the law required that federal officials aid slave catchers in the capture of fugitives. Further, the law instructed that anyone who aided an escaped slave or interfered with the capture of a fugitive was liable for criminal prosecution. Finally, African Americans accused of being runaways

A Southern Abolitionist

In addition to Northern abolitionists, there were Southerners who also opposed slavery. One such was North Carolinian Hinton R. Helper, who argued for emancipation. Helper, referring to himself as "we," wrote:

> The causes which have impeded the progress and the prosperity of the South, which have dwindled our commerce, and other similar pursuits, into the most contemptible insignificance; sunk a large majority of our people in poverty and ignorance, rendered a small minority conceited and tyrannical; entailed upon us a humiliating dependence on the Free States; disgraced us in the recesses of our own souls; and brought us under reproach from all civilized and enlightened nations—may all be traced to one common source—*Slavery!*
>
> Reared amidst the institution of slavery, believing it to be wrong both in principle and in practice, and having seen and felt its evil influence upon individuals, communities and states, we deem it a duty to use our most strenuous efforts to overturn and abolish it! Then we are an abolitionist? Yes! in the fullest sense of the term. We are not only in favor of keeping slavery out of the territories. . . . We here unhesitatingly declare ourself in favor of its immediate and unconditional abolition, in every state where it now exists.

Hinton R. Helper, *The Impending Crisis of the South.* New York: Burdick, 1857, pp. 25–26.

could not speak in their own defense in court, nor did slave catchers have to offer any proof beyond an accusation that a black man or woman was a fugitive. As a consequence, many free blacks were sent south into slavery.

Bleeding Kansas

In 1854 Congress, upon the urging of Illinois senator Stephen A. Douglas, passed the Nebraska-Kansas Act, which revoked the

Missouri Compromise. Although Douglas was against slavery, he wished to lure settlers into the Kansas and Nebraska territories, which lay in the non-slave portion of the old Louisiana Purchase land. Now, not only the New Mexico Territory but any western territory, no matter whether north or south of the old dividing line, would be free or slave depending upon the decision of the territorial legislature.

Douglas's hope was that the majority of the new settlers would be antislavery, as would any new states. His hope did not come true. Kansas, in particular, became a bloody battlefield, where anti- and proslavery supporters killed each other, sometimes individually and sometimes in pitched battles. It soon became known as Bleeding Kansas.

Dred Scott

As war raged in Kansas, a case landed in the Supreme Court that gave slave owners increased rights. In the 1840s army surgeon John Emerson took his slave Dred Scott to various postings in non-slave parts of the United States. Eventually, Scott was sent to Missouri, where Emerson's wife lived. There, he sued for his freedom on the basis of his having lived in the free Minnesota Territory.

After losing his suit in the Missouri state courts, Scott gained a hearing before the Supreme Court in 1857. Again, he lost. However, the Court did not stop with Scott but expanded its ruling, decreeing that the federal government could not ban slavery in any part of the western territories, which meant that slavery could

The Supreme Court's decision in *Dred Scott* makes front page news in *Frank Leslie's Illustrated Newspaper* in 1857.

legally be spread to any part of the West. The ruling also denied that free blacks had any right to U.S. citizenship, a blow to those abolitionists seeking civil rights for African Americans.

John Brown

Both the Fugitive Slave Act and the *Dred Scott* decision enraged slavery opponents. The poet William Cullen Bryant observed that "slavery, instead of being what the people of the slave states have hitherto called it, their peculiar institution, is a Federal institution, the common patrimony [inheritance] and shame of all states."[9] In response to the act and the court decision, abolitionists in many New England towns held meetings to discuss their states seceding. Although some abolitionists like Garrison and Phillips were serious about what they called disunion, others saw disunion not as a serious proposal but as a means of highlighting the central problem: slavery. Abolitionist William Jay wrote that "I rejoice in every exposure of the demoralizing influence of the Union. I rejoice in such exposure, not as tending to bring about dissolution, but to render it unnecessary."[10]

Another response to what abolitionists saw as the caving in of the federal government to slave interests was that of John Brown. His goal was to arm slaves and then carve out a free state in the mountains of Virginia and Maryland. Brown had been active in Kansas, where in response to an 1856 attack on Lawrence by proslavery raiders, he and some followers rode into slaveholding territory and kidnapped five men, none of whom had a hand in the Lawrence raid. Brown killed all five anyway.

Although short on recruits, both black and white, on October 16, 1859, Brown led a raid on the federal arsenal at Harpers Ferry, Virginia. His purpose was to seize weapons, but the raid failed, leaving six of the townspeople and ten of the attackers dead. Brown was captured, convicted of murder and treason, and hanged on December 2, 1859. To many Northerners he was a hero, while to most Southerners he was a villain.

After Harpers Ferry and with the continuing efforts of abolitionists, Southerners were increasingly convinced that it was only a matter of time before the North tried to force the elimination of slavery. Southerners saw abolitionists as dominating the Northern political landscape, when in fact they did not. However, the per-

John Brown and his followers take a stand in the raid at Harpers Ferry.

ception was enough to encourage Southerners to talk seriously of secession. For the South the 1860 election, in which the Free-Soiler—and to Southern minds antislavery—Abraham Lincoln won the presidency, was the final straw. Beginning with South Carolina in December 1860, most of the Southern states seceded, and the stage was set for war and the next act in the drama of abolition and emancipation.

Chapter Two

Emancipation on Hold

Many abolitionists celebrated the secession of Southern states. To them secession took most of the slaveholding states out of the Union, and with these states much of the moral taint of slavery. When war finally broke out in April 1861, most abolitionists reconsidered their stance on secession, concluding finally that the war was necessary because it provided a means by which slavery could finally be ended.

However, neither preceding the war nor after its start were abolitionists satisfied with the stance of the newly elected Abraham Lincoln. The new president had no intention of letting the seceding states remain outside the Union, even if it meant retaining slavery in the United States. Nor when war came was the ending of slavery Lincoln's goal. Rather, he and his administration wished only to restore the Union, again even if it meant accepting a slaveholding South.

Abolitionists and Disunion

William Lloyd Garrison, Wendell Phillips, Frederick Douglass, and a number of other prominent abolitionists could see no reason why the federal government should make any attempt to stop the Southern states from seceding. They believed that the United States should allow a peaceful parting, what they labeled as disunion. Historian James M. McPherson writes:

> The basic Garrisonian argument for disunion was a simple one. Under the Constitution the national government was pledged to protect slavery. The number of slave states had increased from six to fifteen during the existence of the Union. Since the adoption of the Constitution, the slave power had marched on from one victory to another until in 1857 a southern-dominated Supreme Court had declared that Negroes were not citizens of the United States.[11]

When the Civil War began, President Lincoln's goal was to preserve the Union, not to abolish slavery.

Garrison and Phillips further argued that not only was the federal government required to tolerate slavery, it was required to protect slavery interests. As Georgian and one-time member of the U.S. House of Representatives Robert Toombs had once remarked, "We have a right to call on you [all citizens of the United States] to give your blood to maintain the slaves of the South in bondage."[12]

The Debate over Disunion

Not all abolitionists embraced Southern secession. A few felt that allowing Southern states to go shirked the responsibility that abolitionists had toward the 3-plus million African American slaves in those states. Abolitionists such as Stephen S. Foster argued that secession removed the slaves from their Northern friends and any aid that Northerners could provide them. Certainly, if the Southern states became a separate nation as they proposed, no one in the United States would have any legal or political means of undermining Southern slavery.

Garrison and Phillips, however, felt that emancipation would follow quickly in the secessionist South. They believed that slave insurrections would blossom and that the South, lacking the backing of Northern military power, would be unable to suppress these revolts. Only later would it become clear that most slaves felt that they did not have the necessary organization and weapons for successful rebellion and were thus not anxious to face the consequences of a failed uprising. Further, time would show that Southern white militias, which would form the core of the formidable Confederate army, had the military expertise and equipment to deal with such revolts.

The Republicans

Most abolitionists might greet Southern secession with cheers, but the same was not true of the new president or many members of his Republican Party. In 1860 the Republican Party was only a half dozen years old, having formed in 1854 from the wreckage of several other political parties, among them the Free-Soil Party. Although many Republicans disliked slavery and a number were abolitionists, the party was not abolitionist but rather Free-Soil.

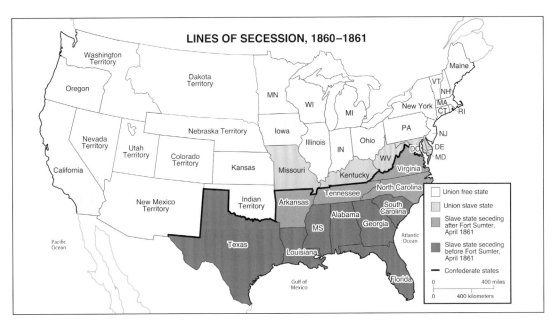

LINES OF SECESSION, 1860–1861

Legend:
- Union free state
- Union slave state
- Slave state seceding after Fort Sumter, April 1861
- Slave state seceding before Fort Sumter, April 1861
- — Confederate states

Thus, much to Garrison's and other abolitionists' disgust, the Republican platform of 1860 did not advocate emancipation, although it did condemn slavery as morally corrupt. The abolitionists also took issue with the Republicans' lack of enthusiasm for African American citizenship and civil rights.

Still, some abolitionists, Frederick Douglass among them, thought the Republicans might mature into a true antislavery party. Certainly, some members of the party, known as Radical Republicans, were abolitionists. However, Douglass was appalled when he discovered that, in order to gain the vote of those prejudiced against African Americans, the party was billing itself as the white man's party, not the black man's. Despite this campaign move, Douglass reluctantly wrote that "I cannot fail to see . . . that the Republican party carries with it the anti-slavery sentiment of the North, and that a victory gained by it in the present canvas[s] [election] will be a victory gained by that sentiment over that wickedly aggressive pro-slavery sentiment of the country."[13] Douglass spoke for many abolitionists who voted Republican in the November 1860 election.

Lincoln and Abolition

Abraham Lincoln, the Republican candidate for president, also came in for his share of criticism from abolitionists, who felt that the Illinois politician was too soft on the issue of slavery. In fact, Lincoln detested slavery. In an 1854 speech he declared:

> I hate it because of the monstrous injustice of slavery itself. I hate it because it deprives our republican example of its just influence in the world—enables the enemies of free institutions, with plausibility, to taunt us as hypocrites—causes the real friends of freedom to doubt our sincerity, and especially because it forces so many really good men amongst ourselves into an open war with the very fundamental principles of civil liberty.[14]

Indeed, Lincoln believed that the country's very existence was threatened by slavery. "'A house divided against itself cannot

Abraham Lincoln

———■———

Born in Kentucky, Abraham Lincoln (1809–1865) grew up on a farm in Indiana. The family had little money, and Lincoln spent far more time working the farm than going to school. His education came from borrowed books.

When Lincoln was twenty-one, he moved to Illinois, where over the next few years he worked as a fence maker, a postmaster, and a surveyor. In 1834 he won a seat in the Illinois state legislature. Intent on preparing himself for his new job, he began studying law and in 1836 passed the bar examination. He then set up a lucrative law practice in Springfield, Illinois.

In 1842 Lincoln married Mary Todd, with whom he would have four children. Five years later Lincoln was elected to Congress, but lost reelection in 1848 because of his opposition to the popular U.S.-Mexican War. In 1858 Lincoln sought the Senate seat of Democrat Stephen Douglas. Lincoln failed in his attempt, but a series of debates with Douglas brought him to national attention. Newspapers all over the country reported on the debates and noted how well Lincoln did in these contests. Lincoln used his new fame to win the Republican nomination in 1860 and then the presidency.

stand,'" he would say, quoting the Bible. "I believe this government cannot endure, permanently, half slave and half free."[15]

Yet despite these feelings, Lincoln believed that legally nothing could be done about slavery within the Southern states since their right to it was guaranteed by the Constitution. However, he was equally convinced that slavery could legitimately be kept out of the new western territories. If slavery could not be eliminated, it could be contained, and eventually, it might wither on its own accord.

Secession

Unlike the abolitionists, Southerners saw Lincoln's election in November 1860 as a victory for abolition, even though Lincoln made it clear in many statements after the election and in his first inaugural address that he had no intention of interfering with slavery in the South. However, he also made it clear that he had every intention of keeping slavery out of the West. To Southerners the new president, no matter what he claimed, was an abolitionist intent on dismantling slavery, and with it Southern society.

In response to the Lincoln election, on December 20, 1860, South Carolina seceded. To justify secession, South Carolinians argued that the U.S. Constitution was a contract between equal partners, the various states, and that any state could withdraw from that agreement at any time if it felt the other parties had violated that compact. South Carolina claimed that the ongoing attempt by Northern abolitionists to end slavery violated the contract between the states.

Over the next month and a half, six other Southern states—Alabama, Florida, Georgia, Louisiana, Mississippi, and Texas—would leave the Union. The remaining four states—Virginia, North Carolina, Tennessee, and Arkansas—would follow in the spring of 1861.

A Southern Constitution and Government

In February 1861 delegates from the seceding states met in Montgomery, Alabama, and drew up a provisional constitution for the Confederate States of America. It was almost an exact copy of the U.S. Constitution. However, unlike that document, the Confederate charter recognized slavery—which, unlike its U.S. counterpart, it did not hesitate to name—and guaranteed the rights of slave owners. For instance, when discussing territorial expansion, the Confederate constitution read: "In all such territory, the institution of negro slavery as it now exists in the Confederate States, shall be recognized and protected by Congress and by the territorial government; and the inhabitants of the several Confederate States and Territories shall have the right to take to such Territory any slaves lawfully held by them."[16] According to historian William C. Davis, "It was probably with no sense of irony at all that immediately after the slave provisions, they appended [attached] the old Bill of Rights."[17]

The delegates also elected a provisional president, Jefferson Davis, and vice president, Alexander Stephens. Both had considerable political experience, having served as senators from their respective home states of Mississippi and Georgia. Of equal importance, both were staunch defenders of slavery and both were slave owners.

Demand for Compromise

Meanwhile, in the North there was a hope that a compromise could be reached that would resolve the crisis peacefully. Most Northerners wanted a return of the Southern states and a restoration of the nation, and for many the presence of slavery in those states was of no concern. Some Northern interests indeed favored retaining slavery. There were banks in New York City who had held mortgages on Southern slaves and did not wish to lose their investments. Wall Street, already the U.S. financial center, feared that the loss of revenues from cotton exports could damage the nation's economy. And textile mill owners in New England did not wish to be cut off from the cotton they needed.

Consequently, beginning immediately after the 1860 election and continuing through the winter of 1861, congressional leaders of the two major parties, Democratic and Republican, looked for a free/slave compromise, much as they had in 1820 and 1850. In order to reach a compromise, most moderate Republicans were willing to accept slavery at least in the South and some even in the West. Only the Radical Republicans were against any compromise with the Southern states if it meant retaining slavery in the United States.

Unlike Republicans, many Democrats were proslavery, either because they came from Southern states that had not yet seceded or because they represented Northern workers and others who opposed black emancipation. But even antislavery Democrats like Stephen A. Douglas were willing to accept the continuation of slavery if that acceptance maintained the Union.

The Crittenden Compromise

In January 1861 Senator John J. Crittenden of Kentucky proposed a package of constitutional amendments that, among other things, would have blocked any interference with slavery within a state by the federal government and protected slavery south of the old 1820 Missouri Compromise line. Additionally, these amendments, known as the Crittenden Compromise, would become a permanent part of the Constitution and could never be repealed by future amendments.

Although Lincoln issued no public statement about the Crittenden Compromise, he let it be known privately to Republican senators that he opposed it. He felt that by passing an amendment allowing slavery in the western territories, Republicans would appear hypocrites and lose all credibility. Lincoln's opposition to the Crittenden Compromise was enough to persuade moderate Republican senators to vote against the proposal, which failed to pass by two votes.

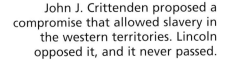

John J. Crittenden proposed a compromise that allowed slavery in the western territories. Lincoln opposed it, and it never passed.

Abolitionism on the Defensive

Abolitionists might be divided as to whether the South should be allowed to leave in peace, but they were united in their belief that no compromise should be made with the South over slavery. Accordingly, they were pleased with Lincoln's firm stand against allowing slavery into the West. Garrison wrote in the *Liberator* on February 15, 1861, that "it is much to the credit of Mr. Lincoln that he had maintained his dignity and self-respect intact, and given no countenance to the compromise."[18] But Garrison and other abolitionists were later disturbed when they discovered that Lincoln was willing to accept a non-repealable constitutional amendment that protected slavery in the Southern states as long as such protection was not extended to the West.

The abolitionists had never been popular with much of the Northern public, and their stand against compromise only increased public dislike of them. The outspokenness of Wendell Phillips and Frederick Douglass, among others, in favor of letting the Union dissolve if it rid the nation of slavery also aroused much hostility. Indeed, angry mobs, made up of those who had investments in the South or who were afraid of economic depression, frequently broke up abolitionist meetings and lectures. These mobs sometimes then roamed about, beating or throwing stones at any African American they met, sometimes entering black neighborhoods where they vandalized houses and stores.

The Opening Shot

With the failure of compromise, war began to appear as the only means of forcing the secessionists back into the Union. And war it was that began on April 12, 1861, when Confederate cannons fired on the Union-occupied Fort Sumter in the harbor of Charleston, South Carolina. With the coming of war, the Northern population that had previously been divided as to its response to Southern secession was now unified in its desire to reunite the country forcefully.

Most abolitionists, even the pacifist Garrison and the fiery Phillips, also dropped their support of secession and embraced the war. Although they recognized that the North was not going to war to emancipate the slaves, they believed that full or partial emancipation had to arise out of the conflict. They were con-

Union troops fire cannons at Confederates during the battle at Fort Sumter, the opening battle of the Civil War.

vinced that, in order to win the war, the Union would have to destroy the slave system. Not to do so would leave the country just as divided as it had been and lead to future conflict. Abolitionists thus envisioned Union armies sweeping down on the South and demolishing its slave society. As Phillips declared in a speech given in Boston nine days after the first shelling of Fort Sumter:

> The hour has struck! Seize the thunderbolt God has forged for you and annihilate the system which has troubled your peace for seventy years! . . . Years hence when the smoke of this conflict clears away the world will see under our banner all tongues, all creeds, all races—one brotherhood— and on the banks of the Potomac, the Genius of Liberty, robed in light, broken chains [of slavery] under her feet.[19]

Douglass Argues for African American Soldiers

■

Although African Americans would eventually serve as Union soldiers, initially they were refused entry into the army. In the following article, the abolitionist and former slave Frederick Douglass argued elegantly in favor of African Americans being enlisted in the Union army.

Why does the Government reject the Negro? Is he not a man? Can he not wield a sword, fire a gun, march and countermarch, and obey orders like any other? Is there the least reason to believe that a regiment of well-drilled Negroes would deport [conduct] themselves less soldier-like on the battle field than the raw troops gathered up generally from the towns and cities of the State of New York? We do believe that such soldiers, if allowed now to take up arms in defense of the Government, and made to feel that hereafter to be recognized as persons having rights, would set the highest example of order and good behavior to their fellow soldiers, and in every way add to the national power.

Quoted in William Dudley, ed., *The Civil War: Opposing Viewpoints*. San Diego: Greenhaven, 1995, pp. 211-12.

Union Yes, Slavery Yes

On July 25, 1861, four days after the Union defeat at the Battle of Bull Run, the U.S. Congress passed a resolution sponsored by Crittenden and Senator Andrew Johnson of Tennessee that made the sole official goal of the war the restoration of the Union. Further, the resolution clearly stated that the federal government was not to interfere in any way with slavery in these states.

Even a number of Radical Republicans voted for the Crittenden-Johnson resolution. They and many abolitionists, as McPherson notes,

at first refrained from open criticism of the government's . . . course toward slavery. Assuming that the "death-grapple with the southern slave oligarchy" must eventually destroy slavery itself, William Lloyd Garrison advised fellow abolitionists in April 1861 to "stand still, and see the salvation of God rather than attempt to add anything to the general commotion."[20]

Military Needs

Lincoln and the moderate Republicans accepted the Crittenden-Johnson resolution because they believed that an antislavery war would be rejected by large numbers of Northerners, and if the United States were to win this war, it was going to need the support of the public, particularly in building a large enough army to ensure victory. Not only would federal troops be facing a large

A Union army colonel leads a group of volunteers into battle. At the start of the war, the Union's military was insufficiently armed and undermanned.

Confederate army, they would also have to conquer and subdue an immense territory about the size of Europe.

At the time of Fort Sumter, the U.S. Army had less than seventeen thousand officers and men, who were stationed at posts scattered across the United States and its territories. Additionally, the army's ranks, particularly among the officers, had been reduced by the resignation of many Southerners. As a result, the bulk of the army would be made up of volunteers and draftees.

Thus, ever mindful of his military needs, Lincoln was very anxious to keep the four remaining slaveholding states—the border states of Missouri, Kentucky, Maryland, and Delaware—in the Union. He feared that any attempt to make emancipation a part of the war's final goal would drive these states into the Confederacy and lose the Union thousands of soldiers who then might fight on the other side. Further, the president knew that many federal soldiers were willing to fight for a restored nation but not for ending slavery.

Filling Out the Ranks

Frederick Douglass and other abolitionists had an answer to the problem of creating a Northern army: African American soldiers. Already, many Northern blacks had tried to enlist in the army, only to be turned away. Douglass pointed out in newspaper articles and speeches that there were thousands of able-bodied men ready to fight for the United States, particularly since the enemy was the slaveholding South. If the goal of the war became emancipation in addition to union, then those thousands might become hundreds of thousands.

Lincoln, however, would not approve the enlistment of African Americans. He still did not want to risk losing the border states, which he believed might bolt from the Union if African Americans were allowed to serve in the army. Also, he felt that many white Northerners would refuse to serve with black troops. And indeed, with racial prejudice widespread in the North, many Union soldiers did dislike the idea. As one New York soldier put it, "We don't want to fight side by side with the negro. We think we are a too superior race for that."[21]

Lincoln's refusal to enlist African American soldiers angered the abolitionists. Once more, the antislavery activists became im-

Sojourner Truth

■

Sojourner Truth (1797–1883) was born a slave in New York State; she was freed by Isaac van Wagener just before New York abolished slavery in 1827. Upon her emancipation she successfully sued to have a young son returned to her after his having been illegally sold south. Moving to New York City, she worked as a servant.

Over the next decade and half, moved in part by religious visions, she became a dynamic preacher dedicated to spreading Christian thought and practice. In 1843 she discovered the abolitionist movement, and bringing skills honed in her missionary work she quickly became one of the movement's most powerful speakers.

During the Civil War, she helped supply African American army units; integrate Washington, D.C., streetcars; and through the National Freedmen's Relief Association counseled former slaves, seeing to the resettlement of many of them. After the war she encouraged large-scale migrations of African Americans into Kansas and Missouri. She also continued work that she had begun in the 1850s to further women's rights.

Sojourner Truth worked for the antislavery cause throughout her life.

patient with what they saw as Lincoln's timidity about emancipation. They would continue to be disheartened by the president's actions over the next year of the war, only to be surprised by Lincoln's later 1862 announcement of the Emancipation Proclamation, the first major step toward the abolishment of slavery and the freeing of the slaves.

Chapter Three

On the Road to Emancipation

Until the fall of 1862, emancipation remained an elusive goal for abolitionists, with Lincoln remaining firm that Southern slavery was not a target of the war. Yet even without intending to do so, the Union was chipping away at the slave system, which was beginning to show cracks under the pressure of war. As author Louis S. Gerteis points out, "Wherever federal troops occupied slave territory, slavery as an institution crumbled and collapsed. While Northerners generally displayed little interest in liberating blacks, federal authorities lacked the will and the ability to maintain or restore the slave system. Emancipation was inevitable, although its details were uncertain."[22]

This halting and undirected emancipation frustrated abolitionists, who argued that a federal policy of emancipation would accomplish two goals. First, it would strip away the major source of labor that the Confederate army depended upon for operations, and second, it would give the war a moral dimension that it lacked. Both arguments eventually swayed Lincoln, whose response was the Emancipation Proclamation, the first major step toward ending slavery and turning the Civil War from a strictly political struggle into a moral endeavor.

A Military Necessity

By the summer of 1861, abolitionists were once more taking aim at Lincoln and his policy, or lack of policy, on emancipation, and they were bringing their message to an increasingly receptive audience. Now that the antislavery activists were supporting the war and the reunification of the nation, they were experiencing a popularity that they had never had in the past. They were also influencing public opinion in ways that had not been possible before. Many Northerners found themselves agreeing with Garrison and his colleagues that the abolishment of slavery would also abolish the division that had led to war.

The abolitionists also promoted another, even more appealing, reason for ending slavery: military necessity. They pointed out that Southern slaves were providing the Confederacy with the means to continue fighting the war. African American slaves worked the fields, built the military installations, delivered supplies, and even worked as nurses in hospitals. Their labor freed up many white Southerners for army duty. The scholar James M. McPherson writes that "there were thousands of slaves doing the heavy physical labor of the southern army . . . allowing soldiers to conserve their strength for the actual fighting."[23]

Black slaves deliver supplies to Confederate soldiers. Freeing slaves became a military necessity for the Union.

Accordingly, the abolitionists argued that it was a military necessity to end slavery and thus to deprive the South of its pool of labor, whose employment was prolonging the war. In the summer of 1861, Frederick Douglass wrote that "the Negro is the key to the situation—the pivot upon which the whole rebellion turns. . . . To fight against slaveholders, without fighting against slavery, is but a half-hearted business, and paralyzes the hands that engage in it."[24]

War Powers

The abolitionists believed that Lincoln had the authority to end slavery in the Southern states. As president he had broad powers in time of war, most notably the ability to order any measure that would cripple the war-making capacity of an enemy. When the secession states had launched the war, they had forfeited any protection of slavery by the Constitution.

Lincoln, however, was not receptive to this line of argument. First, he did not wish to issue an order that he could not enforce. Second, he was afraid that, as long as the border states retained slavery, they would be enraged by any attempt to interfere with slavery in the Confederate states.

Lincoln was not averse to emancipation and hoped to persuade the border states to give up slavery. However, instead of executive or congressional action that might be constitutionally suspect, Lincoln proposed to reduce slavery in the Union gradu-

Fugitive slaves arrive at Union lines. The Emancipation Proclamation gave courage to thousands of slaves to leave their owners and follow Union troops.

ally by paying slave owners for freeing their slaves. Most abolitionists opposed gradual emancipation as unworkable and compensation as rewarding immoral behavior, and they continued to call for immediate emancipation of at least Confederate slaves under the president's war powers. Lincoln's lack of enthusiasm for their proposal frustrated them.

Contrabands of War

While Lincoln and the abolitionists were wrangling over the extent of his war powers, slavery was presenting Union commanders with a dilemma: what to do about fugitive slaves that made their way to Union lines. Initially, neither the Lincoln administration nor army command issued any instructions on how to handle runaway slaves.

General Benjamin Butler found his own solution, and it was one that would be adopted by other federal officers. In May 1861 Butler took command of Fortress Monroe, a military post in eastern Virginia still in federal hands and not far from the site of the original British colony of Jamestown, where the first slaves were landed in 1619. On the evening of Butler's first day in Virginia, three slaves appeared seeking asylum and offering to work for the federalists. Butler needed laborers to help shore up Monroe's defenses, so he took in the fugitives as well as other slaves who appeared.

Not long after, the owner of the first three slaves arrived at the fort and requested their return under the Fugitive Slave Act. In the early months of the war, Union officers assumed that, since they had received no instructions to the contrary, they were to honor this act, as many did by returning fugitives to their Confederate owners.

Butler, however, refused to return the slaves, declaring that each was a contraband of war, which is property or material that can be used by an enemy during wartime. Contraband became the general term applied throughout the war to any Confederate slave in Union hands. By labeling the fugitive slaves as contraband, Butler felt he had a legal right under military law to retain them, particularly since some of them had been used in putting up Confederate fortifications in the area.

Lincoln and his cabinet reluctantly approved Butler's actions, although when the general tried to discover whether his contrabands were free or still slaves, he was unable to obtain a response from the administration. Still, what was beyond doubt was that Butler's contrabands were no longer part of the Southern slave system and no longer aiding either directly or indirectly the Confederate war effort. Further, the general's action set a precedent that other Union officers followed, many taking fugitive slaves under their protection by labeling them as contrabands of war.

The First Confiscation Act

In August 1861 Butler finally received an answer of sorts to his question about his contrabands when Congress passed the First Confiscation Act. The act stated that ownership of contrabands used directly to help the Confederate war effort was nullified, that is, canceled. Such contrabands were no longer slaves, although the act said nothing about whether they were actually free.

Senator John J. Crittenden of the border state of Kentucky objected to the Confiscation Act, claiming that Congress had no authority to pass laws affecting slavery. Supporters of the act argued that Congress did have the right to confiscate the property of those engaged in treason—and rebellion was certainly an act of treason—and that the act was thus aimed at such individuals, not at slavery itself. In the end the act passed with all but six congressional Republicans, including most Radicals, voting for it. All but three Democrats voted against it, setting up a congressional split on the issue of slavery that would last until the end of the war.

The Confiscation Act was only a very small step in the direction of emancipation, if at all, since nothing in the legislation prevented title of contrabands from being restored by congressional action at the end of the war. Still, it was the first federal action that imposed any limits for any reason on slavery since the 1820 Missouri Compromise.

Military Emancipation Decrees

The Confiscation Act did not just apply to slaveholders in Confederate territory but also to slave owners in border states who actively helped the Confederacy wage war. With this in mind, on August 30, 1861, General John C. Frémont, military commander of Missouri, issued a decree that confiscated all property of any Missourians who were Confederate sympathizers, whether they

General John C. Frémont issued a decree that confiscated all property of Confederate sympathizers in Missouri.

were actually helping the South or not. The property included slaves, who were then set free.

Frémont, a popular figure because of his youthful explorations of the American West and his role in winning California from Mexico, had been the Republican candidate for president in 1856 and was a committed abolitionist. He saw the Confiscation Act as a means of pushing forward emancipation as well as crippling Confederate activity in Missouri. However, he had acted without President Lincoln's authorization. Indeed, Frémont had not even notified the president. As Lincoln wrote, "I was stunned. I hadn't authorized Frémont to issue that decree. It went far beyond the first confiscation act, which held that only slaves employed *in the enemy war effort* were to be seized. . . . Slavery was a political matter; decisions about it had to be made by the president and Congress, not by commanders in the field."[25] Lincoln at first requested that Frémont modify his decree to conform to the law, but when the general refused, the president ordered him to do so.

Frémont was not the only army commander who sought to broaden the scope of the First Confiscation Act. In May 1862 General David Hunter, stationed on the islands off the South Carolina coast, declared that all slaves in South Carolina, Georgia, and Florida were free. Lincoln only discovered Hunter's act when he read of it in the newspaper. He immediately countermanded Hunter's declaration.

Presidential Caution

Abolitionists found Lincoln's actions toward both Frémont and Hunter discouraging. For them the two generals had acted rightly and heroically, and Lincoln by reversing them had tossed aside op-portunities that should have led to a more extensive emancipation.

However, Lincoln as always felt that caution was needed. He did not wish to risk further splitting the country by alienating the border states, as he remained devoted first and foremost to restoring the Union. He believed that restoration could be undermined by a too-hasty action against slavery. And in fact, border state slave owners were upset by these sweeping decrees of Frémont and Hunter, deluging Lincoln with angry demands of assurance that the federal government had no intention of interfering with slavery. Reassurances by Lincoln were viewed with suspicion, and constant rumblings of discontent, distrust, and calls for secession continued to issue from Missouri and Kentucky in particular.

An Act of Emancipation

In his nullification of Hunter's decree, Lincoln urged the border states to immediately adopt his program of gradual, compen-sated emancipation. However, there was little interest from

The Emancipation Proclamation

The Emancipation Proclamation, which took effect on January 1, 1863, was the first major step leading to full emancipation and the end of slavery. The proclamation states:

> On the first day of January, A.D. 1863, all persons held as slaves within any State or designated part of a State the people whereof shall then be in rebellion against the United States shall be then, thenceforward, and forever free; and the executive government of the United States, including the military and naval author-ity thereof, will recognize and maintain the freedom of such persons and will do no act or acts to repress such persons, or any of them, in any efforts they may make for their actual freedom.

Quoted in Henry Steele Commager, ed., *Fifty Basic Civil War Documents*. New York: Van Nostrand Reinhold, 1965, p. 72.

Union slave owners for this proposition and no acceptance of Lincoln's program.

The abolitionists for their part continued to reject Lincoln's emancipation plan. However, despite their distaste for compensation, they did cheer when Congress sent a bill to Lincoln abolishing slavery in Washington, D.C., by guaranteeing slave owners three hundred dollars per slave. Since the District of Columbia was not a state, slavery there was not protected by the Constitution. Lincoln signed the bill into law on April 16, 1862. Although the number of slaves emancipated were only a few hundred, it was the first official act of emancipation by the federal government and was celebrated as a landmark event for many years thereafter by African American Washingtonians.

Antislavery Fever

By 1862 the Republican-controlled Congress had become convinced that slavery was the driving force behind the war, and thus, in addition to the D.C. abolition act, it passed a number of laws aimed at limiting slavery. In March it passed legislation forbidding military officers from returning fugitive slaves, and in June it outlawed slavery in all the western territories. Then in July it passed a Second Confiscation Act that clearly stated that contrabands of war, which now numbered in the tens of thousands, were free whether they had engaged in war activities or not.

Lincoln signed all of these measures into law, except the Second Confiscation Act, which he vetoed for being too sweeping and too vague. Congress overrode the veto.

Rethinking Emancipation

Congress's more aggressive stance toward slavery reflected the increasingly antislavery mood of Northerners. In light of this new national mood, Abraham Lincoln was also rethinking his position on emancipation, although he kept his thoughts private, only sharing them with his cabinet. He had concluded that there was much merit in the military necessity argument for emancipating Confederate slaves. He was still uneasy about the constitutionality of the action, but he had already used his war powers to suspend one constitutional guarantee, that of the writ of habeas corpus, a constitutional protection against unlawful arrest and detainment. Thus he concluded that he could suspend a second provision, at least as it applied to the rebel states.

Lincoln was still worried about the reaction of the border states but less so than earlier in the year. The slaveholders in these states had not accepted his program of gradual, compensated emancipation and did not appear to be planning to do so. Also, the Union military's hold on these states was much more secure than in the past.

Therefore, by the summer of 1862, Lincoln had come to believe that at least partial emancipation was possible and desirable. He accordingly drafted a document, later to be known as the Emancipation Proclamation, which would free any slaves of any state still in rebellion on January 1, 1863. It would not, however, free slaves in Union states or in Union-controlled areas of the South, such as the city of New Orleans, which were deemed no longer to be in rebellion. Still, on paper the proclamation would release millions from slavery.

Timing the Announcement

Lincoln now had to decide when to announce his proclamation. To make the proclamation seem more than an empty gesture, the president felt he needed to issue it after a Union victory. However, during the summer of 1862, at least in the East, which both sides considered the heart of the conflict, Union forces were being bested by Confederates under the leadership of Robert E. Lee. Indeed, Lee steadily advanced north and by September was in Maryland, in striking distance of Washington, D.C.

On September 17 the Union and Confederate armies met at Antietam in Maryland. Antietam was an indecisive battle with no clear winner. Still, it did put an end to Lee's northern invasion and sent him back into Virginia. Therefore, Lincoln, in need of a Union victory, declared it one. Five days later, the president issued the Emancipation Proclamation.

Northern Reaction to the Proclamation

Abolitionists and Radical Republicans were stunned and pleased by Lincoln's proclamation and could hardly believe that the man who had been politely but firmly ignoring their calls for such action had finally come around to their point of view. They still were not convinced of his desire for universal emancipation, but they were

Abraham Lincoln writes the Emancipation Proclamation.

nonetheless pleased. Their only fear was that the ever-cautious Lincoln would either water down or refuse to issue the proclamation on January 1, 1863. They were thus relieved when Lincoln did not back down even in the face of criticism north and south.

The general public's reaction to the proclamation was mixed. Some approved of the measure, while others thought it a mistake that would incite slaves to rise up and massacre white Southerners.

The same mixed reaction was present in the army. One New York soldier wrote that Lincoln's proclamation "creates quite a stir in our camp among the officers and men. Some are rejoicing over it, while others are threatening to abandon the service, declaring that they came to fight for the Union and to maintain the Constitution."[26]

Reaction in the border states and among proslavery Democrats was predictably harsh. Those angered by the proclamation charged that, in issuing it, Lincoln exceeded his constitutional authority. To these critics the proclamation was an act of high injustice. As the *Louisville*

Slaves celebrate their liberation. The Emancipation Proclamation gave slaves their freedom.

Daily Democrat wrote, "The President's Proclamation has come at last. We scarcely know how to express our indignation at this flagrant outrage of all constitutional law, all human justice, all Christian feeling."[27]

In the end, most Northerners accepted the coming liberation of Southern slaves, and any number joined in the celebrations by antislavery folk when the proclamation became official. The border states remained in the Union. And most soldiers continued to serve in the Union army because many recognized that Lincoln was acting at least in part to undercut the Confederate ability to fight. Others genuinely despised slavery and gladly fought to end it.

Southern Reaction to the Proclamation

In the Confederate states, white Southerners were enraged by the Emancipation Proclamation. They felt first that it was an illegal act by what they considered a foreign government, and second they feared that it would encourage slaves to run away or even to revolt. Confederate president Jefferson Davis wrote that "Lincoln's so-called emancipation proclamation was the most execrable [terrible] measure recorded in the history of guilty man."[28]

Lincoln, of course, had little to fear from hostile Southern reaction to the proclamation. In fact, the more violent the language and the more heated the defense of slavery, the better it was for him in making slavery a target of war.

Foreign Reaction to the Proclamation

Lincoln was, however, concerned with how the proclamation would be received in Europe, particularly by Great Britain and France. From the beginning of the war, the Confederacy had been trying to persuade one or both of these powers to recognize the South as a sovereign nation and to provide military and other aid. Davis and others knew that the Revolutionary War had been won because of an American alliance with France.

Escaping Bondage

The following letter, written in 1862, is from John Boston, a slave who successfully escaped across the Union line.

> My Dear Wife, it is with grate joy I take this time to let you know Whare I am. I am now in Safety in the 14th Regiment of Brooklyn. This Day i can Adress you thank god as a free man. I had a little truble in giting away But as the lord led the Children of Isrel to the land of Canon So he led me to a land Whare fredom Will rain [rule] in spite Of earth and hell. . . . I am With a very nice man and have All that hart Can Wish But My Dear I Cant express my grate desire that i Have to See you. I trust the time Will Come When We Shal meet again.

Quoted in Ira Berlin, Barbara J. Fields, Thavolia Glymph, Joseph P. Reidy, and Leslie S. Rowland, *The Destruction of Slavery*. Cambridge, UK: Cambridge University Press, 1985, pp. 357–58.

Slavery had been abolished by both Great Britain and France decades before, and neither country wished to be seen helping a slaveholding power. However, as long as the American Civil War remained a political struggle, British and French leaders might eventually be willing to back the Confederacy; the British in particular depended on Southern cotton for their large textile industry.

Foreign reaction to the proclamation was initially lukewarm but quickly grew enthusiastic, especially in Great Britain. The U.S. minister to England wrote that "it is quite clear that the current is now setting very strongly with us among the body of the people."[29] To promote recognition of the Confederacy now meant being proslavery, a position from which British politicians hurriedly distanced themselves, as did their counterparts in France. The proclamation thus effectively ended the South's appeal to Great Britain and France for recognition and aid.

A Union soldier explains the Emancipation Proclamation to a roomful of freed slaves.

Douglass on Lincoln

◼

Many abolitionists were fearful that Lincoln would not actually put the sanctions of the Emancipation Proclamation into effect. However, when he did not back away from those sanctions, many critics became supporters, as is seen in the following writing of Frederick Douglass.

> This noble act completely changed my opinion of the president. I told my friends, I told my readers, I told my neighbors: Abraham Lincoln might be slow, Abraham Lincoln might desire peace without removing our terrible national sore, to fester on for generations, but Abraham Lincoln was not the man to reconsider, retract, and contradict words and purposes solemnly proclaimed over his official signature. His torturous road to this decree was itself a guarantee against retraction. No, Abraham Lincoln would take no step backward. His word had gone out over the country and the world, giving joy and gladness to the friends of freedom and progress wherever those words were read, and he would stand by them and carry them out to the letter. If he had taught us to have confidence in nothing else, he had taught us to have confidence in his word.

Quoted in Stephen B. Oates, ed., *The Whirlwind of War: Voices of the Storm, 1861–1865.* New York: HarperCollins, 1998, p. 237.

Impact on Slaves

The people most affected by the Emancipation Proclamation were of course the millions of African Americans enslaved in the Confederacy. Initially, Lincoln's act had little effect on the lives of these Southern slaves, who continued to work in the fields and homes of their white owners. Many did not even hear of the proclamation until years after its issuance.

Yet as word of the document spread into the South, slaves began making their way to the Union lines in the knowledge that

An illustration entitled *The First Vote* depicts former slaves voting in elections for the first time.

once they reached those lines, they would be free. Also, as the war progressed and Union armies captured Southern land, slaves there automatically became free.

The Importance of the Proclamation

The Emancipation Proclamation certainly did not abolish slavery in the United States, let alone immediately in the secessionist

South, but it was a major step in that direction. The contrabands now were clearly free men and women, and they numbered in the thousands. As more and more Confederate territory came under Union control in the remaining years of the war, the number of emancipated grew. And it would pave the way for passage of the Thirteenth Amendment and the true end of slavery.

The Emancipation Proclamation accordingly elevated the war to a higher moral plane, since the conflict would provide relief from bondage and the suffering of millions of people. Thus in the end, Lincoln was able to sum up the importance of his proclamation by saying that it was "the central act of my administration and the greatest event of the nineteenth century."[30]

The Emancipation Proclamation had another important provision in it. In it Lincoln called for the enlistment of African Americans as soldiers in the Union army: "I further declare and make known that such persons of suitable condition will be received into the armed services of the United States to garrison forts, positions, stations, and other places, and to man vessels of all sorts in said service."[31]

For many African Americans, soldiering would allow them for the first time to attack and help destroy Southern slavery. Additionally, military service might be a way to convince an often racist Northern public that African Americans were ready and able to assume the responsibilities of citizenship.

Chapter Four

Working Toward Emancipation

Despite its limitations, the Emancipation Proclamation was seen by many as the death knell of slavery. Much still needed to be done to make sure that slavery in its entirety was eliminated from the nation, but antislavery activists were encouraged by new state constitutions in the border states of Maryland and Missouri that abolished slavery.

However, an important part of the emancipation for many abolitionists was bringing African Americans into the mainstream of U.S. society. Even in the non-slave states of the Union, black men and women were marginalized and discriminated against. According to historian James M. McPherson, "Abolitionists could not hope to revolutionize the southern social order without first improving the status of northern Negroes."[32]

Consequently, as part of their fight for emancipation, antislavery activists struggled to reform Northern laws. They also believed that enlistment of large numbers of African American men into the Northern army would demonstrate that blacks were committed to the Union cause and should be rewarded for that commitment with fair treatment.

Northern Racism

There was no doubt that large numbers of Northerners held the same racist views of African Americans as those in the South. The scholar Robert R. Durden observes that "differences between North and South in fundamental matters concerning the Negro . . . [was] a matter of differences in degree, not in kind."[33] Feelings against blacks often ran high, particularly among poorer working whites who saw African Americans as potential job rivals. These whites were already upset by the free blacks living in the North, and they had no desire to see Southern slaves freed, as these might pose a further threat to employment. Thus many white laborers resented not only the war but the federal draft that might at any time sweep them into the army and into a war whose goal now was clearly to end slavery along with saving the Union. This resentment boiled over in riots, but none matched the scale of the 1863 draft riot.

The Draft Riot

On Sunday, July 12, 1863, a week after the Battle of Gettysburg ended in Union victory, the worst riot in the history of the United States broke out in New York City. For four days mobs of angry working-class men and women roamed the streets. They burned federal buildings, particularly draft offices. They attacked any newspaper office, such as that of the *New York Tribune*, that supported the war and promoted abolition.

African Americans were one of the chief targets of the rioters. The mobs lynched half a dozen blacks and beat up many more. They wrecked black homes and property and even burned one African American orphanage to the ground. As the *New York Tribune* wrote, "Resistance to Draft was merely the occasion of the outbreak; absolutely disloyalty and hatred to the Negro were the moving cause."[34]

The New York police force, unable to control the rioting, asked the army for help. Several regiments were ordered to New York, arriving on July 15. The soldiers, veteran combat troops, opened fire on the rioters, their deadly rifle volleys having much the same effect on the mobs as they had had on charging Confederates at Gettysburg. Within a day the riot was over. The final death toll was well over a hundred.

Serving the Union

■

The following *New York Tribune* account of the First South Carolina regiment, led by Colonel Thomas Higginson, was among many that commented positively on the conduct of African Americans serving in the Union army. Such reports went far in undercutting the critics who opposed such troops.

> The bravery and good conduct of the regiment more than equaled the high anticipation of its commander. The men were repeatedly under fire; were opposed by infantry, cavalry, and artillery; fought on board of a steamer exposed to heavy musketry from the banks of a narrow river—were tried in all ways, and came off invariably with honor and success. They brought away property to a large amount, capturing also a cannon. . . . Col. Higginson says: "No officer in this regiment now doubts that the key to the successful prosecution of this war lies in the unlimited employment of black troops."

Quoted in Ford Risley, ed., *The Civil War: Primary Documents on Events from 1860 to 1865.* Westport, CT: Greenwood, 2004, pp. 203–4.

Northern Discrimination

Although violence as seen in the New York draft riot aimed at free blacks in the North was all too common, it was by no means the only sign of Northern racism. In many Northern states, blacks could not live in white neighborhoods, attend white churches or white public schools, enter theaters or restaurants, shop in white-operated stores, or stay at hotels. If they were allowed to ride public transportation, they had to ride in segregated compartments or ride on outside platforms. Black orphans were even turned away from white orphanages, and the ill were denied access to hospitals.

African Americans were also barred from practicing skilled trades, such as printing and carpentry. Finding it difficult to receive a decent education, few blacks became doctors or lawyers.

Most African Americans were thus forced to take the lowest-paying jobs.

Black poverty made it necessary for many Northern African Americans to live in the worst housing, often in the most unsanitary conditions. The latter led to much disease and death, particularly among infants, with large numbers perishing each year.

In Ohio free African Americans could only settle in the state if they had five hundred dollars to pay for their care in case they could not support themselves. In neighboring Indiana free blacks were banned altogether. Illinois, Wisconsin, and Minnesota also had varying degrees of these black exclusionary laws, as they were known.

Without Rights

Few Northern states recognized blacks as citizens, and thus routinely denied them any civil rights. In most Northern states, blacks could not vote. In New York only those African Americans with $250, a substantial sum in Civil War America, were allowed to vote; white citizens faced no such financial requirement. Massachusetts and the other New England states, except Connecticut, were the only states that allowed their black residents to vote without any qualification other than residence.

African Americans suffered with other restrictions as well. Even in states where they could vote, they generally could not hold public office, either at the local, state, or federal level. They could not serve on juries. Nor could they testify against whites at a trial. Thus if robbed or beaten by whites, black Americans could not testify on their own behalf; they could therefore be victimized with relative impunity.

Redressing Wrongs

While still lobbying for full emancipation of all African Americans, a number of abolitionists began to attack these fundamental issues of liberty in the North. They agreed fully with the words that abolitionist Edmund Quincy had spoken around 1840: "While the word 'white' is on the statute books of Massachusetts, Massachusetts is a slave state. While a black man can be turned out of a car in Massachusetts, Massachusetts is a slave state."[35] To Civil War abolitionists, all Northern states were thus "slave" states.

Success in correcting the wrongs done African Americans was haphazard but in some cases noteworthy. Although school desegregation failed in most Northern cities, efforts to allow African Americans full access to public transportation, a necessity for getting to and from work without either walking or hiring a carriage, brought reform to public transit policies in New York, Philadelphia, and other Northern cities.

Other reforms followed. McPherson writes that

Congress and northern states enacted legislation that began to break down the pattern of second-class citizenship for northern Negroes: admission of black witnesses to federal courts; repeal of an old law that barred blacks from carrying mail; . . . repeal of black laws in several northern states that had imposed certain kinds of discrimination against Negroes or barred their entry into that state. . . . Perhaps the most dramatic symbol occurred . . . [when] Senator Charles Sumner presented Boston lawyer John Rock for admission to practice before the Supreme Court and Chief Justice Salmon P. Chase swore him in. There was nothing unusual in this except that Rock was a black man, the first Negro accredited to the highest Court.[36]

In the minds of many, however, the right to vote was the most crucial right denied African Americans. To win this right would be a battle that would require further effort and not succeed until five years after the end of the war with the passage of the Fifteenth Amendment.

A Call to Arms

Despite Northern racism with its prejudicial laws and practices against them, many African Americans realized that they had to cast their lot with the Union. For all of its faults, the Union was more likely to end slavery and to offer emancipation than the South.

Additionally, African Americans took heart from Lincoln's call for black enlistees. They, along with many abolitionists, felt that military service would be a chance to show that they were worthy of being citizens with full rights, that like white Northerners they too could risk their lives to bring about a Union victory. According to the scholar Claude H. Nolen, one white officer of the One Hundredth U.S. Colored Infantry told his troops that "their recognition as men would follow their service as soldiers" and that he believed that they would show that each would make "a good citizen."[37]

Slave Life During the War

■

The following is part of the June 1863 testimony of a former South Carolinian slave before the American Freedmen's Inquiry Commission. It provides a picture of the life African American field hands led in the South.

Q. How many hours a day did you work?

A. Every morning till night—beginning at daylight and continuing till 5 or 6 at night.

Q. But you stopped for your meals?

A. You had to get your victuals standing at your hoe; you cooked it overnight yourself or else an old woman was assigned to cook for all the hands, and she or your children brought the food to the field.

Q. You never sat down and took your food together as families?

A. No, sir; never had time for it.

Q. The women had the same day's work as the men; but suppose a woman was in the family way was her task less?

A. No, sir; most of times she had to do the same work. Sometimes the wife of the planter learned the condition of the woman and said to her husband you must cut down her day's work. Sometimes the women had their children in the field.

Quoted in Ira Berlin, Thavolia Glymph, Steven F. Miller, Joseph P. Reidy, Leslie S. Rowland, and Julie Saville, eds., *The Wartime Genesis of Free Labor: The Lower South*. Cambridge, UK: Cambridge University Press, 1990, pp. 250–51.

A recruitment poster solicits black soldiers to fight in the Union army.

To Carry the Fight to the South

Proving themselves worthy of citizenship was of course not the only reason, and perhaps not even the main reason, for African Americans' enlisting in the Union army. Many of the men who signed on were former slaves, large numbers of them recently escaped from the South, and they wanted to strike a blow against slavery and the slave owners.

Frederick Douglass, who was particularly enthusiastic about African Americans fighting for the Union, gave voice to this desire to hit back at Southerners and their slave society. In the March 1863 issue of the *Douglass' Monthly*, in an article titled "Men of Color, To Arms!" he wrote:

> In good earnest then, and after the best deliberations, I now for the first time during the war feel at liberty to call and counsel you to arms. By every consideration which binds you to your enslaved fellow country-men, and the peace and welfare of your country; by every aspiration which you cherish for the freedom and equality of your-selves and your children; by all the ties of blood and identity which makes us one with the brave black men fighting our battles . . . , I urge you to fly to arms and smite with death the power that would bury the government and your Liberty in the same hopeless grave.[38]

African Americans in Uniform

By October 1862, a month after the announcement of the Emancipation Proclamation, wholesale recruiting of African Americans was underway. Over the next two and a half years, some 180,000 black men would serve in the Union army; of that number 120,000 were former slaves. These men would fill the ranks of over one hundred units of infantry, cavalry, and artillery.

However, the proclamation did not mark the first formation of African American combat units. Some Union field commanders had already raised a few such units. In the South Carolina Sea Islands, just off the coast of that state, General David Hunter in April 1862 had asked permission of the War Department to form a black regiment from former slaves. Not receiving an answer, Hunter went ahead but, unable to obtain any funds, had to disband the unit. After the proclamation he was able to re-form the regiment.

In August 1862 General Benjamin Butler, who the year before had first declared fugitive slaves contrabands of war and who was now military governor of New Orleans, began recruiting free Southern African Americans for what he called native guard units. The native guards would soon include former slaves as well as free blacks and would be the first black units to see combat.

Policy and Prejudice

All of these African American units had white officers because the War Department restricted blacks to the enlisted ranks, that is, sergeant and lower. The army, under order of Congress, also paid African American soldiers less than white troopers.

Black soldiers were annoyed at not being able to serve as officers. However, they were far more angry at the inequality of pay. Some even felt that they would prefer not being paid at all to being humiliated by being offered lesser wages than their white counterparts.

In August 1863 Frederick Douglass arranged a meeting with Abraham Lincoln to discuss these matters. Lincoln promised to push Congress to equalize the pay of black and white soldiers. It took almost a year, but in July 1864 Congress set the pay for all privates at thirteen dollars per month, raising it soon thereafter to sixteen. Higher ranks received more, but still equal, pay.

As to the matter of black officers, Lincoln admitted the justice of the request. However, he told Douglass that getting acceptance of blacks in uniform, particularly by many white soldiers, had been difficult enough and that under the circumstances black officers were just not possible.

Indeed, there was widespread prejudice against African Americans in the Union army. Some white soldiers bitterly resented having to serve with blacks, even though whites and blacks were never in the same regiment. Many officers were also hostile to the idea of African American soldiers, and initially, some stated that they would not lead black troops. Nevertheless, as Nolen writes, "by Mid-April 1863, officers who had earlier declared that they would never serve with black troops had come to accept them.[39] And by the end of the war, at least one African American received a battlefield promotion to lieutenant.

Bravery Under Fire

In the spring of 1863, African American troops saw their first combat when Butler's native guards made two heroic, although fruitless, attacks against Port Hudson, Louisiana. In this and some 450 other engagements, African Americans showed that, despite unequal pay and the hostile attitudes of some white soldiers and officers, they would fight well and bravely. Of the Thirteenth U.S. Colored Infantry, for instance, General George

An illustration depicts the storming of Fort Wagner and the death of Colonel Robert Gould Shaw, who led one of the first African American regiments in the U.S. Army.

Thomas wrote that they showed "bravery, tenacity, and deeds of noble daring."[40]

Of the African American regiments, one of the earliest and most famous was the Fifty-fourth Massachusetts Infantry. Initially commanded by Colonel Robert Gould Shaw, a member of one of the most active antislavery families in New England, its members included two sons of Frederick Douglass.

Despite the good combat record of the Louisiana native guards at Port Hudson, Shaw had difficulty winning the right for his men to fight. Finally, on July 18, 1863, the Fifty-fourth Massachusetts joined the attack on Fort Wagner, near Charleston, South Carolina. At the head of the attacking federals, the Fifty-fourth took heavy casualties while pressing the attack, thus proving that African American soldiers were as brave and capable as any of their white companions.

Among those killed in the assault was Colonel Shaw, who was buried in a mass grave with his men. This burial was meant as an insult by the Confederates, angry about the Union using blacks in combat. Shaw's parents, though, were pleased, saying that their son would have wanted to be buried with the men with whom he had served and died.

The South Reacts

The outrage of Fort Wagner's defenders was typical of the response of Southerners to the North's use of African American troops. Confederates felt that arming blacks, many of whom were escaped slaves, was criminal. As a result of this anger, Confederate secretary of war James A. Seddon ordered that captured black Union troops be treated as rebellious slaves and be executed: "They cannot be recognized in any way as soldiers subject to the rules of war and to trial by Military Courts; . . . summary execution must therefore be inflicted in those taken."[41]

Seddon's policy was never implemented, in part because the Union threatened to begin executing Confederate prisoners in retaliation. Additionally, many Southern whites still holding fast to their idea of the happy slave believed that the African Americans serving in the Union army had been conned into service by wily and unscrupulous abolitionists.

Massacre at Fort Pillow

Despite the Confederate government's backing off its execution order, there were cases of the killing of captured African American soldiers and sometimes their white officers. The most notorious instance was the Fort Pillow massacre.

On April 18, 1864, Confederate troops under the command of General Nathan Bedford Forrest overran and captured Fort Pillow in Tennessee. Among the fort's garrison was a black regiment, and when the African Americans attempted to surrender, many were gunned down by the Confederates. Forrest apparently did not order the killing, and he put an end to it as soon as he could, but by then 80 percent of the black troops were dead.

New Yorkers protest the Northern draft by destroying an African American orphanage in 1863. Even in the North, the idea of fighting for emancipation irritated many whites.

Harriet Tubman

■

Like a number of other African American antislavery activists, Harriet Tubman (ca. 1820–1913) was born a slave. In 1849 she escaped from a Maryland plantation. A year later she returned to help her family escape. Over the next decade, she aided over three hundred others to flee bondage, earning her the title of the "Moses" of her people. Noted for her military-like planning and for the discipline she maintained among the parties she helped to freedom, she was sometimes referred to as General Tubman. During this period she met and was befriended by many leading abolitionists.

For much of the Civil War, she worked for the Union army in South Carolina as a laundress and a nurse. Federal officers sometimes used her as a spy: She would enter Confederate territory, where she picked up information among South Carolinian slaves. For all of this work, she was eventually awarded a federal pension in the 1890s, but not before she had spent decades living in poverty.

Harriet Tubman was dubbed the "Moses" of her people, helping many black slaves escape into Northern territory.

A Southern Black Regiment

Despite the massacre at Fort Pillow and several other such incidents, white Confederates were not necessarily opposed to African American troops—if they were fighting for the South. By 1864 high casualty and desertion rates had left the Confederate army seriously undermanned. In January 1864, in response to this personnel drain, Confederate general Patrick Cleburne proposed that slaves be drafted to fill out the ranks. These slaves would be offered freedom for their service.

The Confederate government rejected Cleburne's proposal, but as 1864 wore on and the Confederate army continued to shrink, the idea resurfaced with Robert E. Lee supporting it. Lee urged the formation of several black regiments, arguing that slaves had been one of the Confederates' major assets, doing labor that freed up white soldiers. Now, they could be employed in another useful military capacity. According to historian Shelby Foote, the Confederate "army, by and large, . . . favored adoption of the measure (144 out of 200 men in an Alabama regiment, for example signed a petition addressed to Congress in its favor, and the proportion was about the same in a Mississippi outfit)."[42]

While Confederate president Jefferson Davis had always been a fervent supporter of slavery and an avid opponent to emancipation, he now found himself having to propose at least a limited form of emancipation if he desired any possibility of winning the war. In short, he faced a desperate situation that called for desperate measures. As a result, in January 1865 Davis asked the Confederate Congress to authorize black enlistment as well as the freeing of those who served.

After a fierce debate, the Confederate Congress agreed to the drafting of slaves but refused to promise them emancipation. A Confederate black regiment was then raised, but the war ended before it ever saw action.

Unlike the Union, which was employing African American troops by early 1863, the Confederate effort to enlist black soldiers was too little too late. Additionally, unlike the North that promised freedom, the South offered its black soldiers nothing in exchange for defending a system that had kept them and their fellows in bondage for centuries. In all likelihood, these African Americans, like other Confederate slaves, would have tried to reach Union lines, where they would have been instantly free and might well have then enlisted in the Union army.

As black and white Union troops pushed their way into the South and toward victory, the question in the North was how to put an end to the slavery that had kept so many in bondage, divided the country, and led to civil war. The answer would lie with the U.S. Constitution.

Chapter Five

Emancipation and Beyond

The struggle for emancipation was far from over with the issuance of the Emancipation Proclamation, as far too many African Americans still remained legally in slavery. The end of the war, however, brought the Thirteenth Amendment to the Constitution that abolished slavery in the United States. In the years following the war, the former slaves, at least the men, received constitutional guarantees of full citizenship and civil rights. However, indifference in the North and hostility in the South would see these rights ignored for a century.

Amending the Constitution

By the beginning of 1864, thousands of Confederate slaves had made their way to Union lines in order to find the freedom promised them under the Emancipation Proclamation, and each of the Union armies pushing into the South soon had its camp of fugitive slaves. Historian Roger L. Ransom observes that "with each group of escaped slaves arriving at the Federal army's lines, the Union commitment to total emancipation became stronger." Yet for all that commitment there was little that

The Thirteenth Amendment

Although it took over a year and half to move through Congress and then through the states, the Thirteenth Amendment was finally ratified on December 18, 1865. Its passage finally abolished slavery in the United States, emancipating all those African Americans who still remained enslaved. The amendment states:

Section 1: Neither slavery nor involuntary servitude, except as a punishment for a crime whereof the party shall have been duly convicted, shall exist within the United States, or any place subject to their jurisdiction.

Section 2: Congress shall have the power to enforce this article by appropriate legislation.

Quoted in Henry Steele Commager, ed., *Fifty Basic Civil War Documents*. New York: Van Nostrand Reinhold, 1965, p. 74.

had legally been done to ensure full emancipation. Ransom continues:

As late as 1864, however, the only formal evidence of that commitment was the Emancipation Proclamation, an executive order that would have questionable force once the war ended. Although few doubted that slaves freed by the armies would retain their freedom, there was considerable concern over those not freed by the proclamation. What if the South were willing to negotiate for peace in return for not freeing slaves still in the Confederacy? What about blacks still enslaved in the Union?[43]

Lincoln and congressional Republicans realized that the only certain way of ensuring an end to slavery was a constitutional amendment. Consequently, in the spring of 1864 Republicans drafted a thirteenth constitutional amendment that would abolish slavery in the United States. Needing two-thirds of each house to be adopted by Congress, on April 8, 1864, the proposed amendment easily passed the Senate by a vote of 38 to 6. However, on June 15 it failed by 95 to 66 in the House, where enough Democrats, those who were proslavery, successfully blocked passage.

The Democrats were defiant because Union victory, an essential element for any universal emancipation, seemed once more to be fading as Union advances ground to a standstill through the spring and summer of 1864 outside Richmond and Atlanta. Northern casualties were rising at an alarming rate, and public support for Lincoln was badly eroded. It appeared likely that in the election that fall, Lincoln would lose his bid for reelection and that a new Democratic administration would negotiate peace with the Confederacy.

The Union army captures Atlanta, an important city of the Southern Confederacy.

The House Approves

However, General William T. Sherman's capture of Atlanta in September ended the threat to Lincoln and the possibility of a negotiated peace. Additionally, the 1864 election brought even more Republicans into the House of Representatives, and it was certain that when these new members took office, they would ensure passage of the Thirteenth Amendment.

Nevertheless, Lincoln and other Republican leaders wished to see bipartisan approval of the amendment and set out to win over

The Most Important Step

■

The approval of the Thirteenth Amendment by the U.S. Congress was greeted by many, such as by the *New York Times* in the following quote, as a crucial step toward a fully democratic nation.

The adoption of this amendment is the most important step ever taken by Congress, and its ratification by the requisite number of States will complete the most important act of internal administration performed by any nation for a hundred years. It perfects the great work of the Founders of our Republic. The national feeling was not strong enough to enable them to abolish slavery at the outset of our [the United States'] career, but although slavery has grown in power with gigantic strides since that time, the growth of the sentiment of nationality has outstripped it, and slavery is now abolished, not only without danger to the Union, but as the only means of preserving and making it perpetual. . . . With the passage of this amendment the Republic enters upon a new stage of its great career. It is hereafter to be, what it has never been hitherto, thoroughly *democratic*—resting on human rights as its basis, and aiming at the greatest good and the highest happiness of all its people.

New York Times, "The Abolition of Slavery," February 1, 1865, p. 1.

enough Democrats from the old Congress to adopt the amendment. By January the Republicans had their majority, and on January 31, 1865, the amendment sailed through the House by 119
to 56.

A huge audience of both whites and blacks, men and women,
watched as the House voted on the Thirteenth Amendment.
When the amendment passed, the scholar Michael Vorenberg
writes,

> for a moment there was only a disbelieving, hollow silence.
> Then the House exploded into cheers. Members threw their
> hats to the roof, caught them, and smashed them against
> their desks. For the lawmakers and for the white observers
> who dominated the galleries, this was the vicarious day of
> jubilee. The normally staid Victorian audience lost its emo-
> tional bearings. Witnesses to the great event roared their
> approval, wept, embraced. . . . Blacks in the audience were
> equally moved, not only by the meaning of the event but by
> the reaction of the whites around them.[44]

Outside, cannons fired a hundred-gun salute, people hugged
each other in the street, and a brass band led a crowd to the
White House lawn, where Lincoln praised Congress for its great
moral victory.

Slavery's End

Congressional approval was only the first step in adding the Thirteenth Amendment to the Constitution. To be ratified, the
amendment needed approval by three-fourths of the states. Many
Republican leaders insisted that this three-fourths had to include
the secessionist states of the South, since it was Lincoln administration policy that these states were still part of the United States.
Thus ratification would need a yes vote from twenty-seven states,
there being a total of thirty-six.

In the nonborder states, ratification came easily in the New
England, midwestern, and western state legislatures. New York
proved more difficult because a strong Democratic minority managed to block ratification. However, following Lincoln's assassination in April, enough of these Democrats, leery of public
reaction in frustrating the desires of the fallen president, changed

their votes and approved the Thirteenth Amendment. Only New Jersey voted against the amendment.

The four border states split on approval. Maryland and Missouri, which had recently adopted state constitutions abolishing slavery, voted for the amendment, while Kentucky and Delaware voted against it.

In the end, for ratification the Thirteenth Amendment needed the approval of five Southern states. Pro-Union legislatures in Arkansas, Georgia, Louisiana, Tennessee, and Virginia provided the needed approval, with Georgia being the final state casting the vote for ratification. On December 18, 1865, eight months after the end of the war, the Thirteenth Amendment became part of the U.S. Constitution, and the goal of emancipation so long sought by Frederick Douglass, William Lloyd Garrison, and countless other antislavery activists, both black and white, was achieved.

December 18, 1865, was the true end of American slavery, but June 19 would become the traditional date for celebrating emancipation. Juneteenth, as it would become known, marks the issuance of General Order No. 3 by Union general Gordon Granger on his arrival in Galveston, Texas, in 1865. This order freed all the slaves in Texas under the authority of the Emancipation Proclamation. These Texas African Americans were the last Confederate slaves freed by Lincoln's proclamation.

The Freedmen's Bureau

Emancipation was only the first step toward a completely new life for the former slaves. Confined to the small world of the plantation upon which they lived and strictly separated from the white society around them, most slaves had led a constricted life of labor. Few had any education; few could read or write. As one former slave observed, "[Freedom] came so sudden on 'em they wasn't prepared for it. Just think of whole droves of people, that had always been kept so close, and hardly left the plantation before, turned loose all at once, with nothing in the world, but what they had on their backs, and often little enough of that."[45]

It was clear that these millions of people desperately needed help in order to adjust to their new life. Consequently, on March 3, 1865, Congress established the Bureau of Refugees, Freedmen,

When General Gordon Granger arrived in Texas he freed all slaves in the state under the Emancipation Proclamation.

and Abandoned Lands, better known as the Freedmen's Bureau. The bureau, run by the U.S. Army and headed by General Oliver O. Howard, was the first federal welfare agency. Its primary mission was to feed, clothe, educate, and find jobs for the emancipated slaves. The bureau, however, did not confine its activities to African Americans but also helped feed and clothe Southern

A primary school for freed slaves in Vicksburg, Mississippi.

whites. By 1865 the South had been ravaged by four years of war, and everyone—black and white—was in need.

The first act of the Freedmen's Bureau was to set up food distribution centers in major Southern cities and towns, from which it gave out some 21 million rations. Its second goal was to find paying work for its clients. As one black woman remarked, "This livin' on liberty is lak young folks livin' on love after they gits married. It just don't work. No sir, it las' so long and not a bit longer. . . . It sure don't hold good when you gits hungry."[46] Fortunately, cotton planters were looking for workers, since after four years of war, demand for cotton was high.

Over the seven years of its existence, the Freedmen's Bureau would aid over a million Southern African Americans and thousands of Southern whites. It set up a thousand schools for African Americans and provided close to half a million dollars to train teachers for those schools. Among the schools it established or aided were all the major African American colleges.

Land Redistribution

The Freedmen's Bureau was also supposed to oversee a redistribution of land, to see that the former slaves received large enough plots to start small farms. For antislavery activists both in and out of Congress, land redistribution was necessary in order to achieve a complete overhaul of Southern society and politics. Among other things, they argued that each plantation be divided up into lots of a few acres, and each plot be given to an African American farmer. With a small farm, most of the former slaves could thus achieve independence by raising enough crops and animals not only to feed a family but also to provide a surplus that would bring in some income. Anything less, the abolitionists and Radical Republicans stated, would only see slavery in a new form: with African American working the large plantations to enrich their old owners. True, the former slaves would have to be paid, but that payment, critics claimed, would undoubtedly be low. Thus, without land redistribution, black slaves would be replaced by black serfs.

Lincoln was opposed to land redistribution, and his opposition once more brought the president and many abolitionists and Radical Republicans into conflict. For Lincoln, ever hardheaded, practical, and flexible, it was enough if Southerners pledged loyalty to the Union and freed their slaves. He felt that depriving them of their property would only make reintegration of the South more difficult.

It was the issue of Reconstruction in the South that Lincoln addressed on March 4 in his second inaugural address. The president urged his listeners, and the nation, to act "with malice toward none; with charity for all, with firmness in the right, as God gives us to see the right."[47] The North was not to seek revenge on the South, and Lincoln viewed land redistribution as revenge.

Land redistribution never did become a part of Reconstruction. It was successfully opposed by Lincoln and then, after his assassination, by his successor Andrew Johnson, a pro-Union Southerner from Tennessee. Indeed, as early as December 1863, Lincoln proclaimed that any Confederate who took an oath of allegiance would receive back all his or her property except slaves. Even the Republican-controlled Congress did not favor land redistribution.

In the end, the Freedmen's Bureau could do little but set up a sharecropping system for Southern African Americans. Black sharecroppers received a small portion of the income brought in by the cotton or other crops that they helped harvest. They also generally were provided with living quarters for them and their families and access to a plantation-run general store. Rent for the quarters and payment at the store came out of their sharecropping income. The latter was normally eaten up by rent and store expenses, thus keeping the sharecropper in poverty and dependent upon the plantation for a living. African Americans were not alone in being imprisoned in the sharecropping system; there were also many poor whites who were forced to sharecrop. The South, at least for a time, had replaced slavery with serfdom.

Voting Citizens

Land redistribution may have failed, but other parts of Reconstruction were more successful: obtaining citizenship and the franchise, that is, the right to vote, for African Americans. Frederick Douglass wrote that "slavery is not abolished until the black man has the ballot. While the Legislatures of the South retain the right to pass laws making any discrimination between black and white, slavery still lives."[48] For Douglass and the other abolitionists, the only protection against such legislation was the African American vote that would allow blacks to resist attempts to legally discriminate against them.

While many, both North and South, not the least of whom was President Andrew Johnson, opposed giving African Americans citizenship and the franchise, the Republican-controlled Congress in the 1866 Civil Rights Act granted citizenship and equal rights with whites to African Americans. To forestall any future legislation that might overturn this law, the Congress then

Confederate soldiers take the Oath of Allegiance to the United States.

adopted two constitutional amendments that would protect African American citizenship and civil rights. In 1868 the Fourteenth Amendment was ratified and gave citizenship to African Americans, and two years later, the Fifteenth guaranteed them the right to vote. In actual fact, only black men were eligible to vote; it would not be until fifty years later, in 1920, that the Nineteenth Amendment would permit women, both black and white, to vote.

Reversals

With the Thirteenth, Fourteenth, and Fifteenth Amendments ratified, African Americans seemed poised to enjoy their citizenship: They voted, held office, set up schools and businesses, and owned property. However, there were many forces arrayed against Southern blacks. Frederick Douglass, among others, recognized that constitutional amendments, laws, and even the best of intentions were not always enough. Writing in 1870, Douglass observed:

> Law on the statute book and law in the practice are two very different things, and sometimes very opposite things.
> . . . The pen is often mightier than the sword and the settled

habits of a nation mightier than a statute. It has been said that no people is better than their laws. Many have been found worse than their laws. It is no unreasonable impeachment to say that the American people, and even the American churches, are far in the rear of the American law in respect to the Negro.[49]

On the federal level, President Johnson balked at protecting the civil rights of African Americans, despite congressional legislation and impending amendments. He vetoed the 1866 Civil Rights Act, which Congress promptly overrode, and he campaigned against the Fourteenth and Fifteenth Amendments. In the end, his relations with Congress became so bad that in 1868 he was impeached and came within one vote of being removed from office.

In the South, on the local level, Southern whites were angered over what they saw as preferential treatment of the former slaves. Such white-supremacy organizations as the Ku Klux Klan, one of whose leaders was one-time Confederate cavalry leader Nathan Bedford Forrest, and the Knights of the White Camellia spread terror, beating and killing blacks and their white supporters.

In 1877 the federal government ceased its efforts at Reconstruction, and consequently, all efforts at fair treatment for African Americans in the South disappeared. White communities required literacy tests and the payment of taxes for voter registration, thus denying blacks their right to vote. Jim Crow laws required racial segregation of all public places—schools, parks, restrooms, even water fountains. African Americans would not begin to regain their lost rights until the civil rights movement of the 1950s and 1960s.

Resolution and Victory

As bad as these restrictions were for African Americans, eventually, they would be defeated. Black Americans would find the way, just as many of them had during the Civil War. As Ira Berlin and colleagues write:

Over the course of the war, the slaves' insistence that their own enslavement was the root of the conflict—and that a war for the Union must necessarily be a war for freedom—strengthened their friends and weakened their enemies.

The Struggle Continues

■

Even as he celebrated the passage of the Thirteenth Amendment, Frederick Douglass wrote of the need to go further than just emancipation.

> There was no denying the importance of this great amendment. . . . But it did not go far enough. It did not provide for the one idea I had presented to the American people for the last three years of civil war, and that idea was clothed in the old abolition phraseology. It was the "immediate, unconditional, and universal" enfranchisement of the black man, in every state in the Union, so that he could vote freely in state and federal elections for candidates of his choice.
>
> "Without this," I argued on the platform, "the black man's liberty is a mockery. Without this, you might as well retain the old name of slavery for his condition; for in fact, if he is not the slave of the individual master, he is the slave of society, and holds his liberty as a privilege, not as a right. He is at the mercy of the mob, and has no means of protecting himself."

Quoted in Stephen B. Oates, ed., *The Whirlwind of War: Voices of the Storm, 1861–1865.* New York: HarperCollins, 1998, pp. 611–12.

Their willingness to offer their loyalty, their labor, and even their lives pushed Northerners, from common soldiers to leaders of the first rank, to do what had previously seemed unthinkable: to make property into persons, to make slaves into soldiers, and, in time, to make all black people into citizens, the equal of any in the Republic. . . . When the deed was done, a new truth prevailed where slavery had reigned: that men and women could never again be owned and that citizenship was the right of all. The destruction of slavery transformed American life forever.[50]

Notes

Introduction: Battling for Emancipation

1. Ira Berlin, Barbara J. Fields, Steven F. Miller, Joseph P. Reidy, and Leslie E. Rowland, *Slaves No More: Three Essays on Emancipation and the Civil War*. Cambridge, UK: Cambridge University Press, 1992, p. 3.
2. Michael Vorenberg, *Final Freedom: The Civil War, the Abolition of Slavery, and the Thirteenth Amendment*. Cambridge, UK: Cambridge University Press, 2001, p. 9.
3. Quoted in Louis Filler, *Crusade Against Slavery: Friends, Foes, and Reforms, 1820–1860*. Algonac, MI: Reference, 1986, p. 259.
4. Berlin et al., *Slaves No More*, p. 3.

Chapter One: Abolitionists, Slaveholders, and Emancipation

5. Steven E. Woodworth, *Cultures in Conflict: The American Civil War*. Westport, CT: Greenwood, 2000, p. 32.
6. Quoted in International World History Project, "William Lloyd Garrison." http://history-world.org/william_lloyd_garrison.htm.
7. David Walker, *Walker's Appeal, in Four Articles; Together with a Preamble, to the Coloured Citizens of the World, but in Particular, and Very Expressly, to Those of the United States of America*. Boston: self-published, 1829, pp. 29–30.
8. James M. McPherson, *Battle Cry of Freedom: The Civil War Era*. Oxford, UK: Oxford University Press, 1988, p. 90.
9. Quoted in Allan Nevins, *The War for the Union*, vol. 3, *The Organized War to Victory: 1863–1864*. New York: Scribner's, 1971, p. 96.
10. Quoted in Filler, *Crusade Against Slavery*, p. 248.

Chapter Two: Emancipation on Hold

11. James M. McPherson, *The Struggle for Equality: Abolitionists and the Negro in the Civil War and Reconstruction*. Princeton, NJ: Princeton University Press, 1964, pp. 31–32.
12. Quoted in Ralph Korngold, *Two Friends of Man: The Story of William Lloyd Garrison and Wendell Phillips and Their Relationship with Abraham Lincoln*. Boston: Little, Brown, 1950, pp. 164–65.
13. Frederick Douglass, *Frederick Douglass: Selected Speeches and Writing*. Chicago: Lawrence Hill, 1999, p. 410.

14. Quoted in Mark E. Neely Jr., *The Last Best Hope of Earth: Abraham Lincoln and the Promise of America*. Cambridge, MA: Harvard University Press, 1993, pp. 39–40.

15. Quoted in David Herbert Donald, *Lincoln*. New York: Simon & Schuster, 1995, p. 207.

16. Quoted in Robert R. Durden, *The Gray and the Black: The Confederate Debate on Emancipation*. Baton Rouge: Louisiana State University Press, 1972, p. 6.

17. William C. Davis, *"A Government of Our Own": The Making of the Confederacy*. New York: Free Press, 1994, p. 87.

18. Quoted in McPherson, *The Struggle for Equality*, p. 31.

19. Wendell Phillips, *Speeches, Lectures, and Letters*, series 1. 1884. Reprint, New York: Negro Universities Press, 1968, pp. 413–14.

20. McPherson, *Battle Cry of Freedom*, p. 312.

21. Quoted in Benjamin Quarles, *The Negro in the Civil War*. Boston: Little, Brown, 1953, p. 31.

Chapter Three: On the Road to Emancipation

22. Louis S. Gerteis, *From Contraband to Freedman: Federal Policy Toward Southern Blacks, 1861–1865*. Westport, CT: Greenwood, 1973, p. 11.

23. McPherson, *The Struggle for Equality*, p. 63.

24. Douglass, *Frederick Douglass*, p. 455.

25. Quoted in Stephen B. Oates, ed., *The Whirlwind of War: Voices of the Storm, 1861–1865*. New York: HarperCollins, 1998, p. 69.

26. Quoted in Allen C. Guelzo, *Lincoln's Emancipation Proclamation: The End of Slavery in America*. New York: Simon & Schuster, 2004, p. 158.

27. Quoted in Guelzo, *Lincoln's Emancipation Proclamation*, p. 188.

28. Quoted in Oates, *Whirlwind of War*, p. 280.

29. Quoted in Bruce Catton, *The Army of the Potomac: Mr. Lincoln's Army*, rev. ed. Garden City, NY: Doubleday, 1962, p. 322.

30. Quoted in Francis Carpenter, *Six Months at the White House with Abraham Lincoln*. 1866. Reprint, Lincoln: University of Nebraska Press, 1995, p. 90.

31. Quoted in Henry Steele Commager, ed., *Fifty Basic Civil War Documents*. New York: Van Nostrand Reinhold, 1965, p. 73.

Chapter Four: Working Toward Emancipation

32. McPherson, *The Struggle for Equality*, p. 222.

33. Durden, *The Gray and the Black*, p. viii.

34. Quoted in Ford Risley, ed., *The Civil War: Primary Documents on Events from 1860 to 1865*. Westport, CT: Greenwood, 2004, p. 237.

35. Quoted in Douglass, *Frederick Douglass*, p. 578.

36. McPherson, *Battle Cry of Freedom*, pp. 840–41.
37. Claude H. Nolen, *African American Southerners in Slavery, Civil War, and Reconstruction*. Jefferson, NC: McFarland, 2001, p. 120.
38. Quoted in Risley, ed., *The Civil War*, p. 200.
39. Nolen, *African American Southerners in Slavery, Civil War and Reconstruction*, p. 121.
40. Quoted in Nolen, *African American Southerners in Slavery, Civil War, and Reconstruction*, p. 132.
41. Quoted in William Dudley, ed., *The Civil War: Opposing Viewpoints*. San Diego: Greenhaven, 1995, p. 233.
42. Shelby Foote, *The Civil War: A Narrative: Red River to Appomattox*. New York: Vintage, 1974, p. 860.

Chapter Five: Emancipation and Beyond

43. Roger L. Ransom, *Conflict and Compromise: The Political Economy of Slavery, Emancipation, and the American Civil War*. New York: Cambridge University Press, 1989, p. 208.
44. Vorenberg, *Final Freedom*, p. 207.
45. Quoted in Ransom, *Conflict and Compromise*, p. 219.
46. Quoted in Ransom, *Conflict and Compromise*, p. 221.
47. Quoted in David Herbert Donald, *Lincoln*. New York: Simon & Schuster, 1995, p. 567.
48. Douglass, *Frederick Douglass*, p. 578.
49. Douglass, *Frederick Douglass*, pp. 606–7.
50. Berlin et al., *Slaves No More*, pp. 75–76.

Chronology

April 12, 1861
War breaks out when Confederate forces fire on Fort Sumter in South Carolina.

August 6, 1861
The First Confiscation Act nullifies ownership of slaves used in the Confederate war effort.

April 16, 1862
Congress abolishes slavery in the District of Columbia.

June 9, 1862
Congress outlaws slavery in the western territories.

July 17, 1862
The Second Confiscation Act frees any Confederate slaves who fall into Union hands.

August 22, 1862
In New Orleans, Union General Benjamin Butler forms several units made up of black troops.

September 22, 1862
Lincoln calls for the enlistment of African American troops.

January 1, 1863
Lincoln issues the Emancipation Proclamation.

May 27, 1863
Black troops take part in the attack on Port Hudson, Louisiana.

July 18, 1863
African American soldiers lead the attack on Fort Wagner, South Carolina.

March 16, 1864
Pro-Union voters in Arkansas ratify a state constitution that abolishes slavery.

April 8, 1864
The U.S. Senate approves the Thirteenth Amendment abolishing slavery.

January 31, 1865
The U.S. House of Representatives approves the Thirteenth Amendment.

March 3, 1865
The U.S. Congress establishes the Freedmen's Bureau.

April 9, 1865
Robert E. Lee surrenders to Ulysses S. Grant at Appomattox Courthouse.

December 18, 1865
Ratification of the Thirteenth Amendment.

For More Information

Books

James A. Corrick, *The Civil War*. San Diego: Lucent, 2003. Filled with illustrations, this book traces the course of the Civil War. It also contains excerpts from period documents, maps, a time line, and a resources list.

Stephen Currie, *A Peculiar Institution: Slavery in the Plantation South*. San Diego: Lucent, 2005. This volume places American slavery in its historical context by describing the growth, practice, and eventual end of slavery in the United States. Included are a time line and a list of books and Web sites that provide further information.

_____, *The Quest for Freedom: The Abolitionist*. San Diego: Lucent, 2005. Presenting the genesis, expression, and legacy of the abolitionists and their movement, this title evaluates the impact that these activists had in both the North and the South. Excerpts from primary sources along with a time line and a resources list augment the discussion.

Jessica Gresko, *Slave Rebellions*. San Diego: Lucent, 2006. Relying and quoting from period documents, this work examines the various slave rebellions such as that of Nat Turner that erupted in the pre–Civil War South and their effects on both Southern and Northern views of slavery and emancipation. Additional features are a time line and a list of printed and electronic resources.

Jim Haskins, *Black, Blue, and Gray: African Americans in the Civil War*. New York: Simon & Schuster Children's Publishing, 1998. This title describes the important contributions that African Americans made as soldiers in the Union army as well as their role in supporting Confederate army units. Enhancing the text are a time line, period photographs, and excerpts from period documents.

_____, *Black Stars of the Civil War*. Hoboken, NJ: Jossey-Bass, 2002. This volume contains short biographies of over twenty African Americans who aided in the struggle for emancipation and equal rights just before, during, and after the Civil War.

Stuart A. Kallen, *A History of Free Blacks in America*. San Diego: Lucent, 2005. This book explores the many roles played by the millions of free blacks between the American Revolution and the Civil War.

Peter Krass, *Sojourner Truth*. Rev. ed. Philadelphia: Chelsea House, 2004. Often using her own words, this title details the life and legacy of one of the most influential nineteenth-century African American women who worked to end slavery and to promote civil rights.

Sharman Apt Russell, *Frederick Douglass*. Rev. ed. Philadelphia: Chelsea House, 2004. This biography, augmented by excerpts from Douglass's own writings and a time line, describes the life and impact of one of the most important of African American abolitionists.

Thomas Streissguth, ed., *Slavery*. San Diego: Greenhaven, 2001. This collection presents the history of slavery through personal accounts of slaves, slaveholders, abolitionists, and outside observers.

Bettye Stroud and Virginia Schomp, *The Reconstruction Era*. Syracuse, NY: Benchmark, 2006. This volume traces the history of Reconstruction, looking at the initial progress made by African Americans in the post–Civil War South and the events and attitudes that eventually undercut that progress.

M.W. Taylor, *Harriet Tubman*. Rev. ed. Philadelphia: Chelsea House, 2004. This biography tells the story, frequently in her own words, of this famous African American woman who, after escaping from slavery, helped many others do the same.

Web Sites

Africans in America: Judgment Day: 1831–1865, PBS (www.pbs.org/wgbh/aia/part4/). This site links to biographies of important figures in the battle for emancipation as well as to samples of their writings.

The American Civil War, Dakota State University (www.homepages.dsu.edu/jankej/civilwar/civilwar.htm). This site contains many links to Civil War sites, with two categories specifically linking to information on slavery and emancipation and on African American soldiers.

The Avalon Project at Yale Law School: Documents on Slavery (www.yale.edu/lawweb/avalon/slavery.htm). This site has numerous links to official documents, both federal and state, concerning slavery. It also provides access to *My Bondage and Freedom* (1855) by Frederick Douglass and *The Narrative of Sojourner Truth* (1850).

Documenting the American South: North American Slave Narratives (docsouth.unc.edu/neh/index.html). This site links to many slave narratives that provide detailed descriptions of African American life under slavery as well as to hundreds of period photographs and drawings.

Freedmen and Southern Society Project, Department of History, University of Maryland

(www.history.umd.edu/Freedmen/ fssphome.htm). This site reproduces a number of period letters, reports, and official documents that detail the life of African Americans during the Civil War.

Teacher Oz's Kingdom of History

(www.teacheroz.com/slavery.htm). This useful site provides links to several hundred other sites covering slavery, the Emancipation Proclamation, African American troops, the Freedmen's Bureau, abolitionists, the Underground Railroad, free African Americans, and numerous period diaries, letters, newspaper stories, slave narratives, and other period writings.

Index

Picture Credits

Cover: © Bettmann/CORBIS

The Art Archive/Culver Pictures, 12

© Delaware Art Museum, Wilmington, USA/Howard Pyle Collection/The Bridgeman Art Library, 9

© Yale University Art Gallery, New Haven, CT, USA/The Bridgeman Art Library, 79

© Bettmann/CORBIS, 60, 73, 87

© Historical Picture Archive/CORBIS, 25

© Medford Historical Society Collection/CORBIS, 83

© CORBIS, 56

Ed Wisniewski/The Gale Group, 26

The Bridgeman Art Library/Getty Images, 22, 39

Hulton Archive/Getty Images, 17, 33, 43, 47, 51, 55, 68, 71

MPI/Getty Images, 41

Time & Life Pictures/Getty Images, 58

Getty Images, 45

Library of Congress, 21, 29, 74

© North Wind Picture Archives, 15, 18, 31, 48, 84

Thomson Gale, 35

About the Author

James A. Corrick has been a professional writer and editor for twenty-five years. Along with a PhD in English, his academic background includes a graduate degree in the biological sciences. He has taught English, edited magazines for the National Space Society, and edited and indexed books on history, economics, and literature. He and his wife live in Tucson, Arizona. Among his other titles for Lucent are *The Civil War: Life Among the Soldiers and Cavalry, The Louisiana Purchase, Life of a Medieval Knight, The Incas, The Civil War, Life Among the Incas, The Early Middle Ages, The Byzantine Empire,* and *The Renaissance.*